Best Practices
Motivation
& Student
Engagement

Creating Power Learners

Linda D. Ventriglia Ph.D.

The Best Practices in Teaching Collection

Best Practices Interdisciplinary Vocabulary Development
   The Rule of Three

Best Practices 21st Century Questioning and Problem Solving
   Infolinking

Best Practices Differentiated Instruction
   The Rule of Foot

Best Practices Motivation and Student Engagement
   Creating Power Learners

Best Practices Interdisciplinary Literacy
   Stoplight Strategies

Best Practices English Language Learning
   A Conversational Approach to Language and Literacy

Best Practices 21st Century Teaching
   The EduRevolution

8th edition
© 2013 by Linda D. Ventriglia, Ph.D.
ISBN 978-1-931277-051

Younglight
EDUCATE
Light Up the Mind

The Younglight logo—a bright sun—represents lighting up the mind through learning. Younglight is committed to accelerating the achievement of all learners through professional development books that give teachers a repertoire of research-based Best Practices in teaching. By providing teachers with a repertoire of instructional strategies, Younglight carries out the promise of its logo, books that **Light Up the Mind.**

Visit younglighteducate.com
to find more educational titles in the
Best Practices series of books.

Preface to the Best Practices in Classroom Instruction Series

Quality Teaching: The Best Predictor of High Student Achievement

Student achievement is based on quality teaching. High-quality teaching along with stimulating interaction between students and teachers ensure all students' academic success. This *Best Practices* classroom instructional series is based on the belief that teachers are the greatest resource available to students today.

Proven research-based *Best Practices* in this series provide teachers with a full repertoire of the instructional strategies needed to create optimal learning opportunities for diverse learners. These instructional strategies increase student achievement by focusing instruction on the content standards which are aligned with state assessments.

The *Best Practice* books and accompanying CDs are the result of ten years of school-based research. Schools that implemented the strategies outlined in the *Best Practices in Classroom Instruction Series* showed significantly greater gains in achievement than schools which were matched for socioeconomic status, percentage of free and reduced lunch, transience, attendance, student population and percentage of English learners. School wide adherence to *Best Practices* teaching—including differentiated instruction aligned to standards-based eight-week benchmarks—resulted in dramatic gains in students' achievement. Academic improvement began when the strategies were first employed, and continued year after year. Schools have achieved gold and distinguished status. Some teachers have become National Board certified.

A BEST PRACTICE SCHOOL: *API GROWTH*

Teachers using *Best Practices* reported that their classrooms were forever positively changed. Students became more engaged in learning. Best Practice teaching strategies challenged students to push the limits of their thinking to higher levels of problem solving. This changed the dynamics of learning in the classroom. Students became more thoughtful about what they were learning. They became more self motivated. As Team Leaders in cooperative groups, students mentored each other. The teacher's role changed from a director of learning to a facilitator of learning.

Best Practice teachers noted that after three years, the teaching strategies and classroom groupings became an integral part of how content was delivered and learned in their classrooms. Teachers at Best Practice schools established a learning community that went beyond their schools. The Best Practice concept of "teachers helping teachers" was implemented as teachers served as coaches and mentors of other teachers. This had a significant impact on teacher empowerment. It was the expertise of teachers reflecting on, modeling and implementing Best Practices that ultimately created success for all students.

Best Practices Motivation & Student Engagement is the third book in the Best Practices series. This book outlines how student achievement is accelerated through motivational techniques and student engagement strategies. These strategies can be used across disciplines to create self-motivated or *Power Learners*. Research studies confirm that students that are engaged in learning retain knowledge better and score higher on high-stakes testing.

Table of Contents

Chapter 1

Motivation and Learning

The Power of Praise

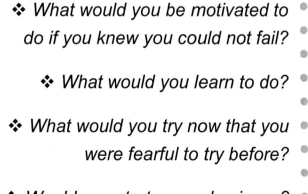

❖ *What would you be motivated to do if you knew you could not fail?*

❖ *What would you learn to do?*

❖ *What would you try now that you were fearful to try before?*

❖ *Would you start a new business?*

❖ *Would you climb Mt. Everest?*

Motivation and Learning

- *What do you think students would be motivated to do if they knew they could not fail?*

- *Would they enjoy learning?*

- *Would they tackle an unsolved math problem?*

- *Would they attempt to find a solution for pollution?*

- *Would they learn a foreign language at an early age?*

- *Would they be anxious to learn algebra?*

Motivation is intricately tied to the learning process. Motivation is defined as "students' willingness, need, desire and compulsion to succeed in the learning process" (Bomia and Belluzo, 1997). Motivation is multidimensional and dynamic.

Motivation is intricately tied to the learning process. Motivation is defined as "students' willingness, need, desire and compulsion to succeed in the learning process" (Bomia and Belluzo, 1997). Motivation is multidimensional and dynamic. It is goal-directed behavior.

Motivation as goal directed behavior can be extrinsic or intrinsic. Students that are extrinsically motivated engage in learning as a means to an end. These students believe that participation in learning activities will result in desirable outcomes such as rewards, teacher praise or avoidance of punishment (Marks, 2001). Intrinsically motivated students, on the other hand, acquire knowledge because learning is satisfying in and of itself. These students engage in learning not because they want a good grade or praise but because they enjoy the process of learning.

Extrinsic and Intrinsic Motivation

Both extrinsic and intrinsic motivation are linked to behavior. Think of students who are highly motivated. They are often described as "hard working" and "well behaved." While these students' behavior is easily described, it is much harder to figure out whether students are extrinsically or intrinsically motivated. Are students working hard because they are motivated to get a good grade or are they motivated to learn for learning's sake alone?

Now think of the students who are labeled "unmotivated." They are described as "disinterested in school, lazy and constantly off task." Even though these students may be disinterested in school, unmotivated is not really an accurate word to describe them. Students described as unmotivated are indeed motivated to do something, even if it is avoiding schoolwork. As long as students choose some goal and expend a certain amount of effort, they are motivated.

The question for teachers is how to get students to become motivated to learn. Research shows that there is no single thing a teacher can do to get students motivated to learn (Biehler and Snowman, 1997). However, there are three approaches to motivation that the teacher may use to create situations that encourage students to want to learn. These approaches are labled: Behavioral, Cognitive and Humanistic.

Mike is a sixth-grade student who is continually off task. He appears unmotivated to learn especially during math time. He puts his head down and rarely participates in discussions. Mike has told the teacher he does not like math and tries to avoid doing it. Mike, however, loves to draw. The teacher, Mrs. Anna Hernandez, is teaching a lesson on fractions. She has students represent fractions on their whiteboards using graphics. At first, Mrs. Hernandez prompts Mike with cues on how to represent the fractions. She praises his implementation of the cues. Mike becomes engaged in the activity. He correctly represents fractions through visual representations. Mrs. Hernandez gives Mike positive feedback each time he gets the right answer. She reinforces the specifics of his accomplishment and prompts him when he needs help. She praises Mike's effort.

Students described as unmotivated are indeed motivated to do something, even if it is avoiding schoolwork. As long as students choose some goal and expend a certain amount of effort, they are motivated.

Mrs. Hernandez, is enhancing Mike's positive self motivation by giving him frequent, positive feedback on relevant math behaviors. She rewards Mike's effort and attributes this effort to his success. She ensures Mike's success with fractions by focusing on Mike's strongest learning modality which is visual. She gives Mike activities that reinforce his proclivity to use this modality to learn fractions.

Mrs. Hernandez uses a Behavioral Approach to Motivation. This approach postulates that positive reinforcement of a behavior causes a student to repeat that behavior. She hopes that by reinforcing Mike's successful behavior in math, he will begin to see himself as a good math learner.

Behavioral Approach to Motivation
The Power of Praise

How do you feel when someone praises how you look or what you have done? Praise does not cost anything, yet it is one of the most powerful motivators. Have you ever told one student, "I like the way you are sitting?" Have you noticed it is like a miracle? Suddenly, the whole class is sitting up straight. This reflects the positive power of praise.

The teacher's well judged, consistent, frequent and targeted use of praise to reward individual or group *effort* on specific behaviors is the most powerful of all positive reinforcers, even more powerful than money (Gawel, 2008). Research states that effective praise is specific and contingent upon the attainment of some standard. It is delivered contingently and continuously until the behavior is learned.

Rewarding behavior is best done in relation to the effort students make in attaining some performance criteria. Praise is most powerful when success is attributed to effort rather than ability (Marzano, 2001). Research has shown that praise that rewards effort can be given by the teacher even after students get the wrong answer. Marzano states that the best way for the teacher to correct mistakes is to: *Pause* and have a discussion with the student on why he or she is having difficulty; *Prompt* the student with a cue on how to improve his or her performance; and *Praise* the student's implementation of the cue as contributing to his or her success (Marzano, 2001).

The Behavioral Approach to motivation confirms the positive power of praise and reinforcement for student learning. It further defines how praise as reinforcement needs to be given. In the beginning students need massed reinforcement of segments of the behavior. Thus, praising students for completing one part of a problem is the first step to students completing the total problem. Once students have been successful completing one learning assignment, they are motivated to continue to complete other assignments successfully.

The teacher's well judged, consistent, frequent and targeted use of praise to reward individual or group effort on specific behaviors is the most powerful of all positive reinforcers, even more powerful than money.

Praise as a Motivator

Motivational researcher Frederick Herzberg found that giving praise or recognition for someone's good work is an effective motivator for continued good work. He found that reinforcement through praise was a powerful motivator for students' learning. Mrs. Hernandez, by giving Mike praise for his visual representations of fractions, motivates Mike extrinsically. She hopes that as Mike gains confidence in math, he will become intrinsically motivated (Gawel, 2008).

Shaping of Behaviors

The question of how to motivate students like Mike was researched extensively by psychologist B.F. Skinner, who demonstrated that students tend to repeat actions that are reinforced (Skinner, 1991). Skinner believed that students' behaviors could be modified by the teacher through the process of continuous reinforcement. It is the process of ignoring undesirable behaviors and reinforcing desired actions that Skinner referred to as *the shaping of behaviors*.

Just as the shaping or sculpting of a piece of art from marble takes time, the shaping of a desired behavior does not occur overnight. The desired behavior must be chunked down and reinforced as partial behaviors at first. The teacher incrementally praises students for each behavioral component that leads to the completion of a learning task. Thus, the teacher through reinforcement shapes the behavior of students to the desired outcome.

Skinner believed that students' behaviors could be modified by the teacher through the process of continuous reinforcement. It is the process of ignoring undesirable behaviors and reinforcing desired actions that Skinner referred to as the shaping of behaviors.

The shaping of behaviors is integral to Skinner's behavioral approach to motivation. Skinner recommends that the teacher use tangible rewards to shape a desired behavior. These rewards can include praise, a good grade or free time to engage in a chosen activity. Skinner postulates that students' motivation is directly related to these tangible rewards.

Skinner extended his behavioral approach from teacher reinforcement of learning behaviors to subject-related programmed learning tasks. Skinner discovered that students learned better when they were reinforced for every correct response. Continuous reinforcement of correct responses motivated students and gave them confidence to go on to the next task.

Many other behavioral researchers have concurred with Skinner that the ongoing acknowledgement of correct answers is important when students are learning something for the first time. These researchers encourage teachers to set up learning situations to facilitate students' success. Teachers are directed to prompt students to choose the correct answers and then to praise them for their choice.

Extrinsic Manipulation of Learning Reinforcers

The Behavioral Approach to Motivation puts the teacher in a position to control the behavior of students by extrinsically manipulating learning reinforcers. It is thought by behaviorists, like Skinner that once learning has been reinforced enough, students may become intrinsically motivated to learn. Thus, Mike may learn to love math because of the positive experiences that Mrs. Hernandez has given him.

Although Skinner placed his emphasis on the teacher's use of positive reinforcers to motivate students, he also acknowledged the role negative reinforcers play in motivation. He noted that negative reinforcers, like staying after school, may indeed curtail a behavior. Negative reinforcers, however, rarely motivate students to engage in learning a subject they have previously disliked or one in which they have previously felt incompetent. Therefore, Skinner cautioned teachers on the excessive use of negative reinforcers. Skinner emphasized instead that teachers should continually focus on motivating students by reinforcing approximations of desired behaviors.

Madeline Hunter, like Skinner, was a behaviorist. She built upon and extended Skinner's research on the shaping of behaviors. Hunter believed that student motivation to achieve in a classroom was directly connected to the use of extrinsic behavioral reinforcers. Positive reinforcers were described as motivators for student engagement in learning. Contrarily, negative reinforcers were noted to have the undesirable side effects of threatening and disengaging learners. Hunter stated:

> *Humans learn best in an environment that is absent from threat, where all the brain's neural energy is used to accomplish the new learning. When threatened, much of that energy is redirected toward survival to get out of the situation that is causing the unpleasant feelings. Students may not be physically threatened in the classroom. They may, however, feel threatened by the humiliation or loss of dignity which has the same negative effect on learning (Hunter and Hunter, 2004).*

The Behavioral Approach to Motivation puts the teacher in a position to control the behavior of students by extrinsically manipulating learning reinforcers. It is thought by behaviorists like Skinner that once learning has been reinforced enough; students may become intrinsically motivated to learn.

It is the teacher's responsibility to establish a learning environment that fosters a sense of community where students feel safe and motivated to learn. According to Hunter, a positive classroom environment is fostered through the teacher's use of five extrinsic behavioral reinforcers: raising the level of concern, feeling tone, success, interest and knowledge of results.

Raising the Level of Concern

The first behavioral reinforcer, *raising the level of concern,* focuses on students' interest or concern about what they are learning. If students are not interested, there will be little learning. When there is too much concern focused on the fear of failing, there is no energy left to focus on learning tasks. A moderate level of concern has been shown by research to best stimulate academic achievement (Hunter and Hunter, 2004).

The first behavioral reinforcer, raising the level of concern, focuses on students' interest or concern about what they are learning. If students are not interested, there will be little learning.

There are a number of ways Hunter suggests that the teacher can raise students' levels of concern moderately. One of the ways is by teacher proximity. This means if the teacher moves and stands next to a student who appears not to be paying attention, the student's level of concern goes up somewhat and he or she usually refocuses on the learning task.

By moving around the classroom and standing next to learners the teacher raises students' levels of concern and increases their on-task behaviors. Besides moving next to students, the teacher can also seat students who continually have trouble focusing, closer to her or him.

Level of concern as a motivator is even more effective when tied to time constraints. This is exemplified in this example: *Maria is not showing an interest in finishing a practice assignment on proposition and support patterns. Mr. William Campo, the teacher, walks over to her and says, "I'll come back in five minutes and check on how you're doing. Remember all the examples need to be finished before the break."*

In this example the teacher raises Maria's level of concern by imposing time constraints. The imposition of time constraints works well with students like Maria who know a skill and are just not motivated. Imposing time limits, however, is counterproductive with students who are having difficulty with a new skill. These students need extra help and time to be motivated to continue. This is apparent in the following classroom scenario.

David is working on two place multiplication. He is having great difficulty implementing on the practice sheet what the teacher taught him during direct instruction. He attempts a problem then looks at the clock. He seems petrified. The teacher, Mrs. Donna Petrie, walks over to David. She explains to him once more the process of two place multiplication. Then instead of leaving David to do the problems himself, she says, "Why don't you work on two of these problems with Edward? Don't worry about finishing the practice page. We will go over two place multiplication again tomorrow."

In this instance, David is not motivated by the teacher's imposed time constraints. He feels so pressured that he cannot do anything but watch the clock. David is motivated by the increased time to work on a couple of problems with the support of a peer. He feels successful as he completes the "chunked-down" assignment.

Celia is a high school student engaged in a group science experiment. After the experiment is completed, individual group members write up a page of their findings. Celia becomes disengaged in learning at this point. She struggles to put down her thoughts. She eventually gives up. The teacher motivates Celia by asking her to work with a partner to write one sentence on the most important finding.

It is evident from these three classroom scenarios that raising the level of concern by using time constraints must be used cautiously. The goal is to raise students' levels of concern, but not to the extent that students cannot function.

Using Feelings for Motivation

The second extrinsic behavioral reinforcer outlined by Hunter to increase motivation is *feeling tone* (Hunter and Hunter, 2004). Recent brain research confirms Hunter's theory that the brain is an emotional structure, not a logical one. Students' feelings about a learning task definitely affect their performance. Feelings can range from pleasant to unpleasant. The more learning is perceived as pleasant, the more students are motivated to perform.

Students' pleasant feelings about learning are also influenced by relationships. Students tend to complete learning tasks to please those they admire and respect. The positive feelings here are related in direct measure to the perceived relationship between the student and the teacher whose reinforcement activity, such as praise or approval, is considered important.

> *Recent brain research confirms Hunter's theory that the brain is an emotional structure, not a logical one. Students' feelings about a learning task definitely affect their performance.*

Jill is never on task. She cleans out her desk instead of paying attention during direct instruction. She rarely completes an assignment. She seems to daydream incessantly. There are times, however, when she is on task and makes an effort. It is during these times that the teacher, Mr. Mike Nota, praises the effort she is making. He walks over and praises her on specific task behaviors. He says, "I like the way you completed the problems in the first row. You've done a great job. It looks like they are all correct." This motivates Jill to continue to the next row of problems.

Rewarding Effort

Rewarding students' efforts to learn, no matter how small, increases their positive feelings toward learning. Students who associate pleasant feelings with learning are more motivated to fully participate in classroom activities.

While pleasant feeling tones have the greatest effect on student motivation, unpleasant feeling tones also serve to activate learners in some instances. Unpleasant feeling tones are usually tied to undesirable consequences as seen in the following example:

Damien is not working on his United States history assignment. He is fooling around and distracting others in his group. The teacher, Miss Clara White, says, "Damien, if you don't get that history task finished, I am going to keep you after school and you will miss your basketball practice."

While Miss White's threat may cause Damien to finish his history assignment, it may also have the negative effect of causing Damien to dislike history. Hunter states that unpleasant feeling tones may have the undesirable side effects of causing students to avoid the content or even the teacher (Hunter, 2004). Therefore, while sometimes it is necessary to use unpleasant feeling tones, it is best to return quickly to positive statements when students begin to put forth effort. Research suggests that praise and other extrinsic positive reinforcers should be given by the teacher in a ratio of 4:1. This means the teacher should give 4 positive reinforcers to every 1 negative.

Success

The third extrinsic motivator is *success*. Have you ever heard the statement, *Nothing succeeds like success?* There has never been a truer statement. Students are motivated when they succeed at learning. They become more motivated when they get problems right. It is a Best Practice to have students always circle the items they got right, rather than those they got wrong.

Success is most potent as a motivator when students have to put forth effort to achieve success. If the task is too easy for students, they experience little success. This is because they have put forth little or no effort. If the task is too hard, students will give up. If the task requires effort, but there is a possibility of success, students become motivated and involved in learning.

Jake is a fourth grade struggling reader. He can decode words but cannot understand the meaning of the words in sentences. The teacher targets important vocabulary words for Jake to study. One targeted word is territory. The next day Jake comes to school with a sweatshirt with the word territory written on it. Jake begins to feel successful in reading. He begins to get excited about learning.

> **Students are motivated when they succeed at learning. They become more motivated when they get problems right. It is a Best Practice to have students always circle the items they got right, rather than those they got wrong.**

Success as a Motivator

Using success as a motivator requires the teacher to differentiate instruction in terms of the assignments she or he gives to students. An assignment that requires no effort for advanced students may require extreme effort for students at lower readiness levels. Students experience success on learning tasks designed to their readiness levels. Therefore, the *Best Practice* teacher must strategically create leveled, differentiated assignments.

Mr. Carl Vang is teaching a group of seventh graders at different readiness levels the English language arts standard: Write research reports. After giving direct instruction on how to write a research report, Mr. Vang differentiates the assignments. He asks more advanced learners to do research on the pros and cons of preserving rain forests. He asks students at lower readiness levels to write a paragraph on rain forests. He helps them forumulate a topic sentence to express their main idea. Then he guides these students through the process of creating graphic organizers. The main idea and significant details of the paragraph are outlined in the graphic organizers. Mr. Vang knows that learning is incremental and that students must master beginning writing skills before they are ready for more advanced writing assignments.

The goal of the teacher is to enable all students to succeed in mastering a learning task. As students succeed at tasks at their readiness level, they feel more motivated to attempt tasks that are incrementally more difficult. The *Best Practice* teacher always keeps in mind that by working with small flexible grouping patterns, he or she can target assignments. Targeted small group learning activities facilitate students' success and motivate them to attempt more and more complex tasks.

The teacher following the Behavioral Approach to motivation manipulates the environment to help students become successful learners. By rewarding effort and incremental success, the teacher uses behavior reinforcers to motivate students' learning. This builds the support base for students to take the risks that lead to future learning success.

> **The goal of the teacher is to enable all students to succeed in mastering a learning task. As students succeed at tasks at their readiness level, they feel more motivated to attempt tasks that are incrementally more difficult.**

Engaging Students' Interest

The fourth extrinsic motivator that the teacher can manipulate is *interest* (Hunter and Hunter, 2004). The Best Practice teacher can capture students' interests by introducing novelty, connecting new concepts to students' background experiences, using students' names, and creating authentic learning activities that relate directly to students' lives.

Motivation is fostered through a combination of using novelty and building upon students' background experiences. Novelty is defined as something unusual. When the teacher introduces something unusual or different in a lesson, this alerts a reflex reaction in students' brains and greater attention results (Hunter and Hunter, 2004). This reflex reaction which elicits attention also happens when learning experiences directly relate to students' background experiences or interests, either inside or outside of school. Brain research confirms that students learn very quickly and easily that which makes sense to them or relates meaningfully to their lives (Zadina, 2007).

The following example reveals how Mrs. Alicia Conejo uses Jose's name and personal interests to get him involved in accomplishing the standard of writing a persuasive essay.

> *Mrs. Conejo is teaching the fifth-grade English language arts standard:* Write persuasive letters and compositions. *She gives examples of persuasive writing by using students' names.* "Jose, think about how you would convince or persuade your parents to buy you a new band instrument. Now let's say, Jose, you had to write a letter to convince your parents. What would you write? What do you think will be your parents' concerns? How will you address these concerns in your letter? Mike and William will you work with Jose to brainstorm a graphic organizer or outline of what Jose should include in the letter to persuade his parents to buy him a new musical instrument?"

Jose becomes extremely motivated in composing a persuasive letter to his parents. He cites all the reasons that they should buy him a new musical instrument. He starts thinking that letter writing is important.

The Best Practice teacher can capture students' interest by introducing novelty, connecting new concepts to students' background experiences, using students' names, and creating authentic learning activities that relate directly to students' lives.

Making Learning Personal

Mrs. Conejo starts the language arts lesson by using Jose's name in a persuasive writing example. Then she makes the learning even more personal by building on Jose's interest in persuading his parents to buy him a new instrument. Because Mrs. Conejo knows that cooperative grouping facilitates learning, she asks Mike and William to brainstorm with Jose on ways he can persuade his parents to buy him the band instrument. She asks the students to brainstorm using a graphic organizer which will form the basis for Jose's persuasive letter to his parents. The persuasive writing assignment, because it is authentic, has great meaning for Jose.

An authentic learning activity extends beyond the classroom to the home and community. Almost all learning can be connected to the world outside of school. Interdisciplinary learning assignments with real world applications can enable students to master history, math and language arts standards. An authentic activity in social science may involve students in comparing the transportation systems today with those used in the 19th century. Students can analyze facts and opinions in advertisements of video games as a language arts activity. A science activity can engage students in the study of genetics as they research their own genetic trees.

An authentic activity is particularly powerful when it relates to a community issue, such as the need for a new playground or for a community park. The teacher can reinforce mathematics standards by having students measure and design a community playground to scale. As students finish their authentic assignments, the teacher needs to give them feedback or *knowledge of results*.

Knowledge of Results

The fifth behavior motivator that can be manipulated by the teacher is *knowledge of results* (Hunter and Hunter, 2004). This is a very powerful motivator for students. The focus here is on the feedback the teacher gives students on their application assignments. Students are motivated to complete tasks when they receive ongoing teacher feedback. Why should students complete homework assignments if the teacher doesn't correct the homework immediately upon its return? Why should students continue to do assignments when they receive back papers covered with red marked corrections and no feedback on how they can improve their writing?

Teachers can motivate students best by giving them specific feedback on *what they are doing well, what they need to improve, and what they specifically need to do to correct their work* (Hunter and Hunter, 2004). Both teacher evaluations and student self evaluations can be used to focus on the specific skills students need to improve.

Ms. Nilda Clark is teaching the English language arts standard: Write simple and compound sentences. After the direct instruction lesson, she asks students to work in pairs to identify and then to create compound sentences. She notices that Sara and Mike are having difficulty. First, Mrs. Clark compliments Sara and Mike for correctly identifying the compound sentences. Then she specifically targets subject and verb agreement as the stumbling block they are struggling with in creating their own compound sentences. This establishes the learning focus the students need to correct their work and motivates them to continue with the assignment.

The teacher can make a tremendous difference in students' desire to learn through the implementation of the five behavioral motivators defined by Hunter, including *raising the level of concern, feeling tone, success, interest* and *knowledge of results*. The Behavioral Approach to Motivation and Learning puts the teacher in the position of environmental manipulator. It is through the teacher's manipulation of students' behaviors that students become actively and positively engaged in the learning process.

> **Students are motivated to complete tasks when they receive ongoing teacher feedback. Why should students complete homework assignments if the teacher doesn't correct the homework immediately upon its return?**

The Behavioral Approach focuses on reinforcing specific student behaviors through giving extrinsic feedback and rewards. The behaviors that are reinforced include students' positive feelings about learning. It is students' feelings that are addressed more explicitly in the Cognitive Approach to Motivation and Learning.

Cognitive Approach to Motivation and Learning Expectations

Look at the sad expression on the face. It reflects the feelings of a student who believes he or she will fail. Because the student believes he or she will fail, he or she generally does. The student feels sad and dejected. Look at the happy expression on the other face. It reflects the feelings of a student who believes he or she will succeed. Because the student believes he or she will succeed, he or she generally does. The student feels confident and happy.

Have you heard these expressions? "If you believe you will be successful, you generally are successful. If you believe you will fail, you generally do fail." How does the teacher create an environment to allow all students to be successful?

The Cognitive Approach to Motivation and Learning is based on the theory that academic performance is related to students' feelings about themselves and their environment.

This means if students believe they are not capable of learning, they won't be capable of learning. If they believe they will fail, they normally do fail. Students' expectations *do* become a reality.

Research done by the cognitive scientists Atkinson and Glasser explains students' motivation for learning as "the need for achievement which is partly innate and partly learned from the environment" (Atkinson, 2004). Students who are motivated to learn usually have had positive experiences. On the other hand, students who have had negative experiences with learning have a fear of failure and, thus, often are not motivated (Glasser, 1986).

Students' positive or negative feelings about learning can also be related to what psychologist Julian Rotter terms locus of control. If students consider success to be related to controllable factors, they will assume responsibility for their success and therefore experience feelings of pride and satisfaction (internal locus of control). If, on the other hand, success is thought to have been brought about by an uncontrollable factor, the student will feel gratitude toward that factor. If failure is viewed by the student as caused by some uncontrollable factor, the student may feel anger or self pity (external locus of control). Thus, the attributions that students make about where control is located in their lives will affect the type and extent of motivation they have toward their studies (Hans, 2000).

Up until the third grade, students who have experienced failure are still motivated to try. They feel that they still have internal control over their learning and can be successful. After the third grade, this is not true. In fact, middle school students who have experienced a long history of failure are likely to feel they are doomed by some external, uncontrollable factors. They thus become unwilling to expose themselves to the risk of trying a new learning task because their predictions are that they will fail.

It is easy to recognize these middle school students in the classroom. They are continually distracting others. They are never on task. They rarely complete an assignment. They refuse to try. These students compensate for their unsuccessful learning experiences by using these avoidance behaviors.

The Cognitive Approach to Motivation and Learning is based on the theory that students' academic performance is related to their feelings about themselves and their environment. This means if students believe they are not capable of learning, they won't be capable of learning.

Glasser (1986) emphasizes that for students to achieve in school, they must have experienced success in one aspect of their lives. Positive experiences at school are important for students' futures. High expectations by the teacher creates the foundation for student success. This coincides with what has been termed the "halo effect" or a self-fulfilling prophecy. If the teacher believes students can learn, they usually do. If the teacher believes students can't master a task, they usually don't.

There are a number of ways that Glasser believes that teachers can turn around students' attitudes about their ability to be successful in school. One of the best ways for teachers to motivate students is to help them achieve one step at a time. Success is not experienced at first in a big chunk; rather it is experienced in small increments.

Chunking Down Tasks for Incremental Success

Have you ever tried to climb 1000 stairs at one time? Was the task daunting? Did you get tired and give up? Would it have been easier to climb 100 stairs each day for ten days? Would you have been successful?

The Cognitive Approach to Motivation encourages the teacher to chunk down learning tasks so that all students can be successful. Like the Behavioral Approach, it reiterates that the most motivating learning tasks are those seen by students as challenging but achievable. The Best Practice teacher chunks down learning tasks so that they are not too easy or too hard.

The goal is to differentiate learning tasks to make all learners feel challenged and motivated. Tasks that set the bar one level higher than students' academic functional levels are the most motivating for students. These leveled tasks guarantee the success of all learners.

Guaranteeing the success of all students then is within the teacher's grasp. The teacher allows all students to be successful by correctly diagnosing students' levels of readiness and then adjusting the difficulty of assignments. If the teacher is instructing students on the language arts standard: *Write a narrative,* assignments may range from writing a paragraph to writing a complete story with the characters, setting and plot. Leveling assignments makes all the difference in students' motivation and success.

Marissa is an eighth grade student who is reading at the third grade level. She has had little success in school. Every time she faces an assignment in her eighth grade history class, she anticipates failure even before she begins the assignment. She is a behavior problem and is often off task. The teacher, Mr. James Sota, adjusts the level of difficulty of tasks so that Marissa will have success. Mr. Sota does this by chunking down the eighth-grade standard: Compare and contrast motivations of characters from different historical eras. He first gives Marissa a paragraph to read at the third grade level on the motivations of 19th century educator Maria Montessori. Mr. Sota has Marissa read him the paragraph and praises her reading. He has her answer questions about Montessori's motivations. He reinforces her correct answers. He then has her read another paragraph on 20th century educator Jaime Escalante. Finally, Mr. Sota has Marissa use a Venn diagram to compare and contrast the motivations of these two educators. Once again, Mr. Sota praises Marissa's accomplishment of making the Venn diagram. Marissa is beginning to have success. She can both read and do the written assignment. Marissa after several successes begins to feel confident enough to take risks in learning.

Tasks that set the bar one level higher than students' academic functional levels are the most motivating for students. These leveled tasks guarantee the success of all learners.

Reinforcing Small Increments of Success

Mr. Sota helped motivate Marissa by giving her small increments of success. He chunked down the eighth-grade standard and praised Marissa's success as she mastered each step. He arranged the learning increments at the appropriate instructional level. Research states that the appropriate instructional level is one where students get correct responses 75% of the time. Students like Marissa who have had a history of failure need tasks on which they can experience a 95-99% success rate (Glasser,1986).

Teachers must also give continued reinforcement to students like Marissa to build a support base that will enable them to become motivated to take risks in learning. By giving Marissa small incremental learning tasks at her instructional level, Mr. Sota builds her confidence and motivation to learn subsequent tasks. It is the success at each incremental step that drives Marissa to be motivated to take the next step in learning.

The Cognitive Approach to Motivation puts the teacher in the position of a facilitator of learning. The teacher guides students to take small steps so they will become motivated to take larger risks.

The Cognitive Approach to Motivation puts the teacher in the position of a facilitator of learning. The teacher guides students to take small steps so they will become motivated to take larger risks. The role of the teacher is to reinforce students' beliefs that they can become successful learners and that "inch by inch learning is a cinch."

The Humanistic Approach to Motivation and Learning extends from the Cognitive Approach. It manipulates the environment to create intrinsically motivated, self-actualized learners. It gives students the responsibility for their own learning.

Students are given the freedom to learn in the way they feel most comfortable. They are guided rather than directed by the teacher to build on what they know and extend their knowledge to higher levels through self-designed learning activities.

Humanistic Approach to Motivation
Need for Belongingness

The Humanistic Approach to Motivation proposed by Maslow complements the Behavioral and Cognitive Approaches by extending extrinsic reinforcers to intrinsic self-directed learning. Maslow (1987) postulated that there is a five leveled hierarchy of needs. The first four needs in ascending order are: physiological, safety, belongingness, love and esteem. The fifth highest level is self-actualization. The teacher's interaction with students facilitates their climb to the top.

Ben is a student in Ms. Terri Wing's high school algebra class. Ben lives in an inner city neighborhood. Ben is being raised by his grandmother who cleans houses to put food on the table for Ben and his four brothers and sisters. Ben appears to be surviving on beans and rice. He is often hungry. He has a limited wardrobe but is always clean. Ben's brother belongs to a gang and there are often shootings in the neighborhood where Ben lives. Ben is always looking over his shoulder when he plays basketball after school in the neighborhood park. He is anticipating the sound of gun shots. Ben's grandmother rarely has time to talk to him. Ben wishes he had a mother and father like his friends. Ben sometimes thinks it his fault that his mother left him and his brothers and sisters.

Ms. Wing notices that Ben often daydreams in algebra class. He appears unmotivated to learn. Ms. Wing believes it is because Ben has not fulfilled the first four needs of Maslow's motivational hierarchy which include: meeting his physiological needs; fearing for his safety in the neighborhood; experiencing a feeling of belonging by receiving attention from his family members; and building self esteem by believing he is a worthwhile individual. Ms. Wing believes unless these lower level needs are fulfilled, it is impossible for Ben to move to the highest level of Maslow's hierarchy which is intrinsic motivation to learn or *self-actualization*.

Maslow postulated that there is a five leveled hierarchy of needs. The first four needs in ascending order are: physiological, safety, belongingness, love and esteem. The highest level is self actualization. The teacher's interaction with students facilitates their climb to the top.

A Hierarchy of Motivation

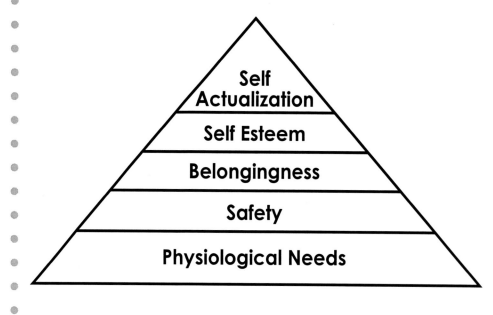

Maslow's Humanistic Approach to Motivation arranges needs in a hierarchy with physiological needs at the base of the triangle and self actualization needs at the top. Maslow initially proposed that unless all the other needs in the hierarchy were met, it was difficult for students to become self-actualized intrinsic learners. Maslow thought that students had to be at the self-esteem level on the hierarchy to move toward self actualization. He later found this was not true.

Maslow discovered through extensive research that students could indeed become self-actualized when their cognitive needs were fostered and developed in the classroom. These cognitive needs included the need to know and understand. Maslow determined that students like Ben could meet the majority of their needs through cooperative group projects. Maslow found that conditions such as the freedom to learn and investigation with peers in cooperative groups facilitated students' self actualization.

In addition to cooperative grouping, a fair and nurturing environment contributed to students becoming self-actualized intrinsic learners. This was true even when their lower needs on the hierarchy were not met. Students who became members of groups fulfilled their needs for safety, belonging and self esteem.

> *Maslow found that conditions such as the freedom to learn and investigation with peers in cooperative groups facilitated students' self actualization.*

Cooperative group learning, according to Maslow, develops the other needs on the hierarchy. Students' safety needs are met as they develop nurturing relationships with their peers. Interpersonal relationships established in cooperative groups fulfill students' need to belong. Self esteem is developed as students make contributions to completing a cooperative group project or assignment. By meeting their needs through the cooperative learning process, students ultimately gain the sense of well being required to self actualize and become intrinsically motivated learners.

Humanistic Approach to Motivation

For Maslow, true motivation to learn was intrinsic. Maslow's Humanistic Approach took issue with Skinner's and Hunter's theory of extrinsic motivators. He believed that the use of external rewards eventually discouraged students. This is because when these were no longer present or became meaningless, there was little desire for students to learn. The extrinsic motivators ultimately replaced students' innate desire to acquire knowledge for its own sake.

By meeting their needs through the cooperative learning process, students ultimately gain the sense of well being required to self actualize and become intrinsically motivated learners.

Essentially, Maslow believed that students' innate desires to learn should be cultivated. Students' growth and development toward self-actualization was fostered through their interactions on targeted learning assignments. The teacher's role was to facilitate the process of classroom groupings.

The Humanistic Approach to Motivation thus addresses learning from the standpoint of students building interpersonal relationships. It strongly promotes cooperative learning groups, rather than competitive, individualistic learning.

Research by Bandura, Marzano and others supports Maslow's premise that cooperative grouping is far superior to individual learning paradigms for increasing students' motivation and learning across the curriculum. Studies found that positive self concepts in specific subjects were related to students working successfully with their peers on learning assignments (Bandura, 1997).

Individualistic vs. Cooperative Learning

Do you think that most students like working alone or in a group? Why do you think that 21st century multidisciplinary learning promotes students working together to solve real world problems? Why is the saying, *two heads are better than one* more fact than fiction?

Why do most classrooms promote individualistic learning goals rather than cooperative learning goals? How are individualistic goals established? What determines students' success?

Individualistic learning structures are characterized by students working alone and earning rewards through the quality of their own efforts. This means that the success or failure of other students is not important. Students are focused on themselves. Learning is competitive. In a competitive system, if students have had a history of success, they usually do well. If students have had a history of failure, the pattern tends to be repeated.

Cooperative learning tasks, unlike individualistic learning tasks, are not based on previous success or failure. Students work together to achieve common learning goals. This means that success or failure is based on the group effort, rather than on the effort of one individual.

Cooperative learning tasks, unlike individualistic learning tasks, are not based on previous success or failure. Students work together to achieve common learning goals. This means that success or failure is based on the group effort, rather than on the effort of one individual. Because all students in the group help each other to successfully complete an assignment, cooperative groups are characterized by positive interdependence (Slavin, 2006).

Cooperative groups foster more motivated learners. Students who are fearful to take risks in learning become more motivated through the support of others in the group. These students convey the belief that "we can do this assignment if we try hard and work together." Students in cooperative groups are thus motivated out of a sense of obligation to help their other team members succeed. Classroom cooperative learning can be likened to athletics where students are motivated to work as a team to win the game.

Cooperative Learning Groups

The teacher can determine the effectiveness of cooperative group activities through assessing these behaviors:

1. Students choose under free-choice conditions to complete assigned learning tasks.

2. Students demonstrate a high degree of effort and perseverance.

3. Students work on learning assignments for long periods of time. They do not quit when they are faced with obstacles.

4. Students' effort and persistence lead to the positive completion of learning assignments (Pintrich and Schunk, 1996).

These behaviors are often seen in cooperative learning groups. Students who are unmotivated to work by themselves, often work wonderfully well with others. Cooperative learning assignments create the conditions in which unmotivated students consistently choose to expend a great amount of energy on positive learning behaviors.

Although the Behavioral, Cognitive and Humanistic Approaches to Motivation don't give the teacher a magic formula, they do suggest ways to engage students in learning. All three approaches confirm the benefit of positive reinforcement to increase motivation. Positive extrinsic reinforcers, whether tangible or intangible, are temporary measures. The teacher's objective is to decrease the extrinsic motivators that are necessary to motivate students.

The ultimate goal is to create intrinsically motivated learners. This goal is addressed in each model through the role of the teacher. The Behavioral Approach to Motivation positions the teacher as the manipulator of the extrinsic factors in the environment. The teacher's role is to extrinsically motivate students using praise and other positive reinforcers. The teacher shapes students' behaviors and motivates students to learn through techniques such as raising students' level of concern, focusing on positive feeling tones, building on success and giving students feedback or knowledge of results. The Behavioral Approach to Motivation postulates that through

> *Cooperative learning assignments create the conditions in which unmotivated students consistently choose to expend a great amount of energy on positive learning behaviors.*

the teacher's consistent implementation of extrinsic rewards, students become motivated. As students experience success, they eventually become intrinsic learners.

The Cognitive Approach to Motivation incorporates environmental extrinsic reinforcers like the Behavioral approach. The difference in the two approaches is how they position the teacher. While the Behavioral Approach positions the teacher as a manipulator of the environment, the Cognitive Approach positions the teacher as a facilitator of learning. The teacher facilitates incremental learning experiences at the levels of students' readiness. He or she reinforces success at every incremental step. It is postulated in the Cognitive Approach that when students continually feel successful, they will become intrinsically motivated.

The Humanistic Approach to Motivation sets forth the belief that it is through the teacher's facilitation of cooperative groups that students reach the highest level of Maslow's hierarchy which is self-actualization and intrinsic motivation.

Finally, the Humanistic Approach to Motivation complements the Behavioral and Cognitive Approaches. The teacher's role is as a facilitator of the cooperative learning process. The Humanistic Approach to Motivation sets forth the belief that it is through the teacher's facilitation of cooperative groups that students reach the highest level of Maslow's hierarchy which is self-actualization and intrinsic motivation.

Think About Discussion Questions

1. Hunter identifies on page 8 five extrinsic behavioral reinforcers that teachers can use to increase students' motivation in learning. Create three additional extrinsic behavioral reinforcers that you can use in your classroom to increase students' motivations to learn and give examples of each.

2. Think about your next unit of study in relation to Maslow's Humanistic Approach to Motivation. Generate some cooperative learning activities that would motivate the students in your class. Implement at least one of these activities. Write a reflection on the effectiveness of the cooperative learning activity using the four behaviors listed on page 25.

Reflection on Approaches to Motivation and Learning

1. Reflect on the role of the teacher in the Behavioral, Cognitive and Humanistic Approaches to Motivation as they are summarized on pages 25-26. How would you analyze your teaching style and your usual classroom grouping patterns? Would you categorize yourself in a Behaviorist role as a manipulator of the environment or in the Cognitive and Humanistic role as a facilitator of the learning process? Give at least two examples that demonstrate how you manifest one of these roles in your teaching style.

2. The Cognitive Approach to Motivation encourages the teacher to chunk down tasks in incremental learning activities to enable students at different readiness levels to be successful. Explain how you would do this in your classroom.

Chapter 2

Ten C's for Developing Intrinsically Motivated Learners

Two Mayans were chipping away at stones.

The first Mayan was asked: *"What are you doing?"*
He hesitated and then said, *"Chipping at this stone."*

The second Mayan was then asked:
"What are you doing?" He replied quickly,
"Creating a powerful pyramid."

To imagine the unimaginable is
the highest form of motivation!

- Are we creating stone chippers or pyramid builders?

- Are we creating learners that are so bored with learning that they continue chipping at the stone without enthusiasm?

- Are we creating pyramid builders who are so involved with learning as a constructive process that they motivate themselves?

- How can we as educators create the conditions that inspire students to motivate themselves?

- What are the Best Practices for motivating students to achieve to their potential academically, personally and socially?

Motivation and Engagement in Learning

High motivation and engagement in learning have consistently been linked to increased levels of student success and reduced drop-out rates (Blank, 1997, Kushman, 2000). Former Secretary of Education Terrell Bell once stated *There are three things to remember about students' success and education. The first is motivation. The second is motivation. The third is motivation.*

> **High motivation and engagement in learning have consistently been linked to increased levels of student success and reduced drop out rates.**

There is no dispute that motivated students learn better. Yet, just how to keep students in school and motivate them to become self directed learners eludes many educators. Numerous studies have shown that students' motivation significantly decreases as they get older (Anderman and Midgley, 1998). By middle school, unmotivated students have poor attendance and early drop-out rates. Students who drop out of school state that school is just not really meaningful to them. They are not motivated to do assignments that are not relevant to their daily living.

Andy, an eighth grade student, has been tested and designated as a gifted learner. You would never know he was gifted by his behavior. He refuses to do his class assignments. He daydreams and doodles incessantly. He wants to become a graphic designer. He is a wonderful artist. He hates school. He does not see the relevance of school to his ultimate goal.

If lack of relevance and meaning are at the roots of student disinterest in school, then it is up to teachers to create more engaging learning environments. The challenge for teachers is to create the educational conditions which will motivate students to expend great energy on behaviors that will lead to academic success.

Research has shown that teachers can create conditions that extrinsically motivate students. School practices that motivate students extrinsically include giving points for completion of assignments, providing tangible rewards and creating privileges on the basis of academic performance (Brooks, 2001).

While external rewards sustain productivity, they reduce student interest in academic tasks. They also reduce students' desires to become independent learners. Students are motivated only long enough to get the reward. (Hunter and Hunter, 2004).

Extrinsic rewards are thus only a partial answer at best for establishing student motivation for learning. A much better answer is implementing open-ended assignments that engage students actively in learning. Meaningful assignments require students to think and make choices. Students become intrinsically motivated when they discover new information with their peers.

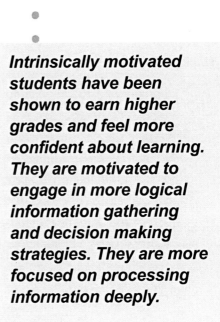

Intrinsically motivated students have been shown to earn higher grades and feel more confident about learning. They are motivated to engage in more logical information gathering and decision making strategies. They are more focused on processing information deeply.

Intrinsically motivated students have been shown to earn higher grades and feel more confident about learning. They are motivated to engage in more logical information gathering and decision making strategies. They are more focused on processing information deeply. Most importantly, these students are more likely to become lifelong learners.

Enhancing students' motivation has long been understood as part of the teaching-learning process. It is, however, the Best Practice teacher's systematic focus on research-based motivational strategies that eventually develops intrinsically motivated learners. *Best Practice Strategies* that increase students' intrinsic motivation in instructional settings include the *10 C's of Motivation: Confidence, Choice, Content Integration, Challenge, Command, Collaboration, Conversation, Constructivism, Creation* and *Celebration.*

Building Confidence: The First C of Best Practice Intrinsic Motivational Strategies

Confidence is the first C of the *Best Practice* intrinsic motivational strategies. The confidence students possess is usually established well before thy enter school. Their confidence is based on the successes or failures they have experienced in mastering a myriad of skills ranging from learning to talk to riding a bike. Even those students who have experienced a number of failures enter school feeling confident and ready to face learning challenges.

After third grade, continual real or perceived failure takes its toll on students. They not only lose their confidence but also their motivation to learn.

Then some students are faced again with the reality of failure. They struggle learning to read. Their underdeveloped vocabulary impedes their comprehension. They are placed in remedial groups. Their confidence is attacked. They begin to think that they aren't good learners. However, despite the failures students experience up until the third grade, they retain their confidence (Kushman, 2000). After third grade, continual real or perceived failure takes its toll on students. They not only lose their confidence but also their motivation to learn.

Sustaining and building *confidence* is therefore the first strategy the teacher uses to increase students' intrinsic motivation. Building confidence, according to Keller, is accomplished by helping students succeed at challenging tasks and providing them with some control over their own learning (Keller, 2004). Confidence is also built by clarifying instructional goals for students and having students set their own goals.

Mrs. Mary Paulson is a third grade teacher. Jaime is a student in her class who is having trouble with mathematics. He cannot read the story problems in the third-grade math text. He struggles with the words. He cannot set up math equations. He is beginning to get discouraged and hate math. His confidence is dwindling. He won't attempt any of the math problems because he believes he will fail. Mrs. Paulson knows that she must build Jaime's confidence. She has a peer read the problems to Jaime.

Then she teaches Jaime the vocabulary words that refer to math operations so he can set up math equations. Jaime chooses three problems for homework that model the words and operations he has learned. Jaime begins to feel that he has some control over his own learning. He gains increased confidence. The fact that he becomes motivated is evidenced by his desire to take math problems home to solve.

Jaime is beginning to become a self-motivated learner. The confidence he is gaining through his success in math is beginning to change his belief that he is a failure. According to motivational research, it is students' beliefs that influence their academic success. When learners believe that their successes are linked to uncontrollable factors, their motivation is lower. On the other hand, when students believe they have control in learning situations, their motivation increases. Mrs. Paulson gives Jaime some control over his learning which increases his confidence. It is students with this confidence that develop into intrinsically motivated learners.

Providing Explicit Choices: The Second C of Best Practice Intrinsic Motivational Strategies

The second C of *Best Practice* intrinsic motivational strategies is *Providing Explicit Choices*. Giving students alternatives to choose from is a *Best Practice* that enhances motivation (Malone and Leper, 2003). Students become more motivated when they are encouraged to explore topics that coincide with their personal interests.

There are two components of students' interest in learning which relate to motivation. These components include feeling-related interest and value-related interest (Schiefele, 1991). Feeling-related interest refers to the degree of enjoyment that students have when studying a given topic. If students enjoy the topic they are studying, they are more motivated to learn. Value-related interest concerns the importance of the learning task. If students think the topic is important, they are more motivated to learn. The Best Practice teacher creates learning experiences that capture both students' feeling-related interests and their value-related interests.

Some learning approaches build on students' interests by encouraging them to make choices. Pedagogy in the Montessori Method is based on the freedom, self activity and self education of the child (Montessori, 1967). Montessori wrote about sensitive periods in young children's learning when they are drawn to opt for activities that accelerate their cognitive development. The Montessori classroom is structured to facilitate the selection process. Students direct their own learning; they decide whether they want to work on the number rods or at the language center. They show great intrinsic motivation.

The Montessori Method focuses both on student choice and teacher-guided choice. The teacher facilitates the learning process by guiding students to move in the direction they need for their academic development. The system of choice advocated by the Montessori Method is important for the Best Practice classroom. The teacher guides students by giving them choices around a specific standard that is to be mastered.

The Montessori Method focuses both on student choice and teacher guided choice. The teacher facilitates the learning process by guiding students to move in the direction they need for their academic development. The system of choice advocated by the Montessori Method is important for the Best Practice classroom.

Mr. Bob Carter is a high school history teacher. He is beginning a unit on American Political life. During direct instruction, he emphasizes the United States history standard: Students evaluate, take and defend positions on the influence of the media on American political life. He tells groups they can choose a viewpoint and defend their position on the influence of the media. Group one takes the position that the press is very good at presenting facts that are important in shaping public opinion of critical issues. Group two decides that there needs to be more restrictions on press releases. They believe the press often presents opinions, rather than facts. They take the position that the media needs to become more responsible. Finally, the third group proposes that new electronic sources, such as the Internet, will have the greatest impact in educating the citizenry on American political life. Mr. Carter has students share their viewpoints with the class. The class then compares and contrasts viewpoints on a graphic organizer.

Mr. Carter's goal is to have his students apply the United States history standard through their research on the role media has had in American politics. He accomplishes this goal by having students choose and defend a point of view on the influence of the media. Students become motivated and engaged in learning as they promote their point of view to others in the class.

Content Integration: The Third C of Best Practice Intrinsic Motivational Strategies

Content Integration is the third C of Best Practice intrinsic motivational strategies. Content integration as a Best Practice is supported by recent brain research. This research affirms that the brain is a natural pattern seeker. There is no computer software that has the pattern recognition of a human being (Zadina, 2007). The brain processes whole and part together. This means that learning is best delivered in an integrated manner. Language arts or math standards are best learned when they are integrated across subject areas, rather than isolated in language arts or math periods. Integrating content across disciplines is a *Best Practice* that motivates students to see patterns and make connections in learning (Keller, 2005).

Ms. Jennifer Lanz teaches eighth grade students in a language arts and United States history block. She takes advantage of the block to reinforce the language arts standards in the context of history. She has taught the following standard in the language arts part of the block: Read expository text. Use word meanings within the appropriate context to show ability to verify those meanings by definition, restatement, example or by comparison and contrast. She has students apply the language arts standard in the history part of the block. Since students are studying about 17th century New England, she has them find recipes from that period. She then has students work in groups to verify unfamiliar words by writing definitions or by restating the language in the recipes.

Ms. Lanz, by teaching the eighth grade English language arts standard on expository reading across disciplines, makes it easier for students to apply the standard. Students come to understand that standards are not isolated skills or concepts. They can be applied across subject areas. Students learn the real life application of the expository reading standard by finding 17th century recipes. Students are more intrinsically motivated to complete assignments when they can see the connection from what they are learning to the real world.

> **Recent brain research affirms that the brain is a natural pattern seeker. There is no computer software that has the pattern recognition of a human being.**

Challenge: The Fourth C of Best Practice Intrinsic Motivational Strategies

Challenging students with skills just beyond their readiness level is the fourth C of *Best Practice* intrinsic motivational strategies. Students become more intrinsically motivated to complete assignments when they are within their reach academically. Flow theory of motivation states that students experience a flow of learning when the challenge of assignments is just above their skill level. The *Best Practice* teacher differentiates assignments to challenge students to move to the next level of skill development (Wang, 2001).

Flow theory of motivation states that students experience a flow of learning when the challenge of assignments is just above their skill level.

Mr. Joe Vento is implementing project-based learning in his high school health classroom. After teaching a unit on nutrition, he puts students in challenge groups. Then he differentiates assignments. He challenges a group at a lower level of readiness to make a list of foods that have been shown to prevent disease. He challenges a group at a higher readiness level to conduct internet research to compare and contrast vegetables and other food products on their potency to prevent different types of diseases in an excel spread sheet format.

Mr. Vento adjusts learning assignments to challenge students at appropriate levels. By adjusting the level of difficulty of assignments, he gets the optimum flow of student motivation and learning. The level of challenge and flow of motivation can be likened to a ladder (Wang, 2001). At the bottom of the ladder is boredom which occurs when students are not sufficiently challenged. At the top of the ladder is anxiety which occurs when the challenge is too great. The flow of motivation occurs in the middle of the ladder at a point where the students' abilities match learning activities. Challenging students at an appropriate level increases their intrinsic motivation for learning.

Command: The Fifth C of Best Practice Intrinsic Motivational Strategies

The fifth C of *Best Practice* intrinsic motivational strategies is *Command*. A *Best Practice* strategy is to give students command over their own learning by creating Team Leaders to direct student groups. Team Leaders are responsible for the management and the discipline of the group. They are also responsible for assigning roles to students and for leading group discussions. Team Leaders work closely with the teacher. They receive group assignments from him or her. They confer with the teacher on learning goals. Students assume leadership roles as Team Leaders to help them become responsible independent and intrinsic learners.

Miss Katy Kelly teaches fourth grade. She uses cooperative learning teams for students to complete assignments. She strategically assigns each group a Team Leader. She explains to the class that the Team Leader is in command as the teacher for the group. Mrs. Kelly has Team Leaders wear badges that say Team Leader to further reinforce their authority.

The teacher meets with Team Leaders in the morning to go over specific class research assignments while the other students do an anchor activity. She has Team Leaders designate specific activities for each member of their group. Students are given roles such as editor, researcher, writer or illustrator. The teacher makes it very clear to student groups that the Team Leader is in command of the group and that questions should be addressed to him or her. If the Team Leader cannot answer the question, it is he or she that confers with the teacher.

Team Leaders who take command for group behavior and learning become more responsible. Even students who frequently show behavior problems often respond well in leadership roles. As Team Leaders become involved in decision making and the organizing of content, they become more intrinsically motivated. They take an active role in their own learning and in the participation of group members.

> **A Best Practice strategy is to give students command over their own learning by creating Team Leaders to direct student groups. Team Leaders are responsible for the management and the discipline of the group. They are also responsible for assigning roles to students and for leading group discussions.**

Collaboration: The Sixth C of Best Practice Intrinsic Motivational Strategies

Collaboration, the sixth C of *Best Practice* intrinsic motivational strategies, enhances thinking and galvanizes students to participate in the learning process. Collaboration promotes problem solving, learner independence and flexible interactions. Research on collaborative learning has identified five defining elements that increase the intrinsic motivation of students. These include:

1. *Positive interdependence (Students are responsible for each other's learning.)*

2. *Face to face interaction (Students serve as facilitators for their peers.)*

3. *Individual and group accountability (Everyone contributes to the learning goal.)*

4. *Interpersonal and small group skills (Students take command of learning.)*

5. *Group processing (Students do self evaluations of learning)* (David Johnson and Roger Johnson, Cooperative Learning Center, 2007)

Collaboration promotes problem solving, learner independence and flexible interactions. Research on collaborative learning has identified five defining elements that increase the intrinsic motivation of students.

Collaborative learning is most effective when it is applied systematically and consistently to classroom instruction (Lou, 2006). The Best Practice teacher uses collaborative or cooperative grouping strategically to accomplish specific learning goals. He or she is also strategic in the assignment of students to groups. Because ability grouping is less desirable than mixed ability groups, the teacher assigns students at multiple readiness levels to groups. The goal is to have students learn from each other. Students are also grouped by interest, common experiences or self-selection.

Mr. Paul Lee is a middle school science teacher. He follows all his direct instruction lessons in science with "hands on" learning labs. Students in groups perform experiments and document their results. At the beginning of the year, Mr. Lee assigns students to groups based on common interests

noted on student surveys. During the first group meetings, he has students discuss their background knowledge and interests in the field of science. This builds rapport among students. It sets the foundation for the science discussions that will become part of their future learning experiences.

Collaboration in learning helps students clarify their thinking and more deeply process information. Face to face interaction encourages students to brainstorm together the answers to questions needed to solve problems and create new solutions. Cooperative grouping works best when students actually depend on each other to reach a learning goal. Rewards are based on group performance.

Students as they collaborate with peers feel a sense of responsibility for the group's success. They need less reinforcement from the teacher. They become intrinsically motivated to learn. As they become intrinsically motivated, students establish their own informal learning networks and self-managed teams that form, operate, dissolve and re-form.

Collaboration in learning helps students clarify their thinking and more deeply process information Face to face interactions encourage students to brainstorm together the answers to questions needed to solve problems and create new solutions.

Conversation: The Seventh C of Best Practice Intrinsic Motivational Strategies

Even though *conversation* is integral to the collaboration process, it is the seventh important Best Practice intrinsic learning motivator in and of itself. Conversation is dialogue. The word dialogue comes from two Greek roots, *dia* and *logos* suggesting *meaning flowing through*. Conversations or dialogue connects meaning between learners. If students have the opportunity to engage in shared conversations related to a particular learning problem over a period of time, they can eventually arrive at the correct solution (Jaworski, 2004).

Dialogue does not require students to agree with one another. Instead, dialogue encourages students to participate in a pool of shared meaning that leads to a particular solution or course of action. Bohm (2008) compares dialogue to *superconductivity*. In superconductivity electrons cooled at a very low temperature flow around obstacles without colliding with one another, creating no resistance and very high energy (Polyektov, 2006). Conversations create the same type of energy as superconductivity. Important insights are gleaned through dialogue. Conversations lead to students putting more energy into the learning process. This leads to intrinsically motivated learners.

English language learners develop academic and social language through the meaningful flow of conversations directed at solving a problem or completing a learning activity.

Conversations are particularly important for English language learners. These students learn language through conversations with their peers (*Ventriglia*, 1992). English language learners develop academic and social language through the fluid meaningful flow of conversations directed at solving a problem or completing a learning activity.

Ms. Katherine Natale is a second-grade teacher who encourages dialogue in all the grouping patterns she uses. This includes paired as well as small-group learning patterns. She knows that conversations are most effective in small groups of no more than four students. Ms. Natale facilitates the conversations in groups by posing questions for students

to answer. Sometimes the questions are a follow-up activity. After the class reads a literature selection on friends, Ms. Natale poses the questions: How do you know someone is your friend? How does a friend act? What does a friend do? Describe your best friend. Ms. Natale knows that questioning is a function of language that is not often developed. She reinforces the English language arts second-grade standard: Respond to questions with appropriate elaboration. She has students write and ask their own questions about friends. She gives English learners the question stems that they can use to formulate their questions. After questions are written, Ms. Natale tells students to discuss their answers with other group members.

Engaging in meaningful dialogue accelerates English language learning. It produces better results than having students answer questions by themselves. Students become more interested when they can share their thoughts with a peer. They are more excited about solving problems. They are not easily discouraged. Ultimately, dialogue becomes an intrinsic motivator for learning.

> **Engaging in meaningful dialogue accelerates English language learning. It produces better results than having students answer questions by themselves.**

Constructivism: The Eighth C of Best Practice Intrinsic Motivational Strategies

Constructivism is the eighth C of *Best Practice* intrinsic motivational strategies. As a cognitive position, constructivism holds that all knowledge is constructed. Constructivism is based on the belief that learning is a natural, continuous process that results in student engagement with the world. In his observations of children, Jean Piaget found that children constructed their knowledge by exploring and experiencing the world around them. Piaget discovered that children first learned about the world by manipulating concrete objects. By manipulating objects and testing hypotheses, Piaget noted that children naturally used a constructivist approach to learning. Constructivism is considered a research-based Best Practice for student motivation. Students who construct their own knowledge are intrinsically motivated to learn.

Mr. Ron Kremer is a third-grade teacher. He believes that students learn best through hands-on activities that require them to construct their own knowledge. He knows that authentic learning experiences give students the opportunity to form important math principles. Mr. Kremer teaches the third grade math standard on measurement and geometry: Choose the appropriate tools and units and estimate and measure the length, weight or mass of given objects. *He has students estimate the length of an earthworm or estimate the weight of pennies in a jar.*

Authentic hands-on activities lead students to formulate and prove hypotheses. As students create the steps to solve a problem, they develop their thinking processes. They also make decisions or choices. Decision-making skills are particularly important. Students must learn to choose among alternatives. They must use logic and precise language to justify their thinking on how to solve a whole range of academic and social problems or challenges. The ability to make inferences requires students to analyze, synthesize and evaluate information. As students implement these skills to construct their own knowledge, they become intrinsically motivated.

> **On Bloom's hierarchy creation is a higher level thinking skill. Creation in and of itself requires intrinsic motivation. Famous artists, inventors and musicians create for the sake of creating. Students get excited about learning when they are given the opportunity to generate and extend ideas, to suggest hypotheses, to apply imagination and to look for alternative innovative outcomes.**

Creation: The Ninth C of Best Practice Intrinsic Motivational Strategies

The ninth C of *Best Practice* intrinsic motivational strategies is *Creation*. On Bloom's hierarchy creation is a higher level thinking skill. Creation in and of itself requires intrinsic motivation. Famous artists, inventors and musicians create for the sake of creating. Students get excited about learning when they are given the opportunity to generate and extend ideas, to suggest hypotheses, to apply imagination and to look for alternative innovative outcomes.

Mrs. Velma Treadwell is a high school science teacher who consistently teaches the science standards using the Teach, Practice and Apply format. Today, during the Teach or direct instruction part of the lesson, she introduces the science standard on ecology which states: Students know how to analyze the changes in an ecosystem. *The Practice part of the lesson engages students in analyzing changes in climate and changes in the environment that affect ecosystems.*

Finally, for the Apply part of the lesson, students participate in a creative activity. Students are asked to create a plan on how to achieve balance in an ecosystem through a balance between competing effects.

Creative thinking skills are crucial for the 21st century. Students living in the 21st century will be bombarded with facts. Information currently doubles every few days. Over 100,000 new pieces of information are received a minute (Futurist, 2009). This information cannot be memorized. It can be used, however, to make inferences and to solve problems. A Best Practice then is to motivate students to sift through data to come up with creative insights and innovative solutions.

Coming up with creative insights using applied imagination is a 21st century skill (Pink, 2006). Creation is tied to idea generation. Brainstorming and creation are linked as ways to address solutions to learning challenges. Synthesizing, a higher level thinking skill, is also tied to creation. The synthesis of ideas is necessary to create something new. In the 21st century, it is creation that needs to take center stage. It is through the process of creation without imposed time limits that students become truly self actualized intrinsic learners.

Synthesizing, a higher level thinking skill, is also tied to creation. The synthesis of ideas is necessary to create something new. In the 21st century, it is creation that needs to take center stage.

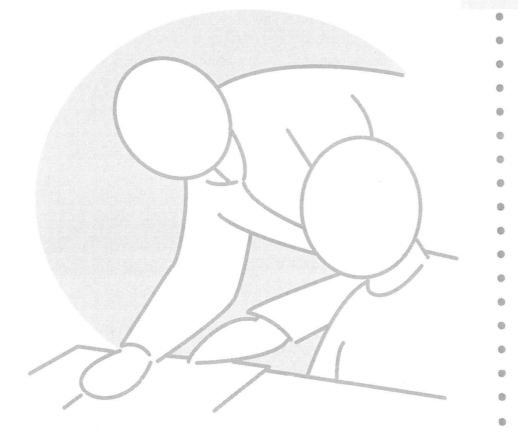

Celebration: The Tenth C of Best Practice Intrinsic Motivational Strategies

The *Celebration* of students' achievements in learning is the tenth C of *Best Practice* intrinsic motivational strategies. Students are motivated to continue learning when their achievements are celebrated. Student work can be celebrated by posting their problem solutions on bulletin boards, arranging presentations at science fairs, publishing essays on Web sites or by using blogging to get feedback from others.

> *Mr. Carlos Gristine is a high school foreign language teacher. He uses technology to celebrate students' progress in becoming bilingual. He congratulates students on their linguistic proficiency through e-mail. He uses blogging to establish a way for students to communicate with each other in the foreign language. He sets up video teleconferences where students can question and respond to issues from their peers in another country who are native speakers. He encourages students to celebrate their fluency in a global language.*

The celebration of accomplishments is most effective when it comes from outside sources as well as the teacher. The use of *blogging* to share student work is a powerful strategy for students' feedback and the celebration of learning.

The *Best Practice* teacher uses the 10 C's for motivation to develop students' intrinsic motivation for learning. By building *confidence* and encouraging students to make *choices* in learning, the teacher develops independent thinkers. Students who are *challenged* at appropriate levels are motivated to continue learning. *Integrating content* across disciplines motivates students to make connections. Having students take *command* of learning teams, encourages students to become leaders. Establishing *collaborative* work groups, motivates students to use *conversations* to share ideas and process information more efficiently. Implementing a *constructivist* approach to learning, motivates students to *create* knowledge through a continuous learning process. Finally, the *celebration* of students' achievements motivates students to become lifelong learners.

Think About Discussion Questions

1. Think about the 10 C's of Best Practice intrinsic motivational strategies in relation to the subject or one of the subjects you teach. Rank the 10 C's in order of importance for students' learning of the content standards. Justify how your highest ranked motivational strategies contribute to your students becoming intrinsically motivated learners.

2. Design an activity for your classroom that will promote *Creation*, the 9th C of Best Practice intrinsic motivational strategies. The activity should involve students in synthesizing data to create something new. Implement the activity and write a reflection on students' motivation.

Reflection on Best Practices for Student Motivation

1. Reflect on the following quote using what you learned in this chapter.

    Motivation is the art of getting students to do what you want them to do because they want to do it. (President Dwight D, Eisenhower)

2. Reflect on specific instances of unmotivated students in your classroom. Describe each experience in detail. Then prescribe some of the 10 C's to develop the motivation of students. Analyze how what you prescribed will develop intrinsically motivated students.

Chapter 3

Motivational Styles of English Language Learners

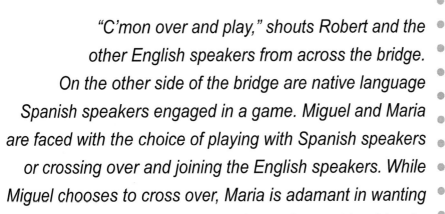

"C'mon over and play," shouts Robert and the other English speakers from across the bridge. On the other side of the bridge are native language Spanish speakers engaged in a game. Miguel and Maria are faced with the choice of playing with Spanish speakers or crossing over and joining the English speakers. While Miguel chooses to cross over, Maria is adamant in wanting to remain with her Spanish-speaking friends.

Motivational Styles and Language Learning

- *Why does Miguel cross over the bridge to interact with English speakers while Maria stays behind?*

- *Does this action mean Miguel is more motivated to learn English than Maria?*

- *Why are some English language learners more motivated to learn the English language than others?*

- *Are students who seek out and exploit language practice opportunities more motivated?*

- *Do English language learners have different motivational styles?*

- *Do personalities and learning preferences play a part in motivational styles?*

- *How can the teacher match instruction to English language learners' motivational styles?*

Research indicates that the strongest motivation for students to learn English as a second language is the perception that their personal abilities will be maintained or improved.

While it is apparent in the example that Miguel is motivated to *cross over* the bridge to interact with English speakers, it is less clear why Maria isn't motivated to *cross over* with him. On the surface Miguel's behavior indicates that he is more motivated to learn English. He goes across the bridge to interact with English speaking peers. He makes use of the learning opportunity to practice the English language.

Research indicates that the strongest motivation for students to learn English as a second language is the perception that their personal abilities will be maintained or improved (O'Houle, 2005).

Research on motivational styles reveals that students' approaches to language learning differ. Some learners like Miguel take an active role in language learning. Others like Maria take a passive approach. Still others vacillate between actively participating in language learning and declining to participate. Usually, the decision whether or not to aggressively pursue language learning opportunities is directly related to students' perceptions of whether or not their personal abilities will be improved. Students who believe that language learning will benefit them personally take an active role. They make use of all practice opportunities to master social and academic language. Students, on the other hand, who don't think becoming bilingual will greatly benefit them, remain passive learners. Finally, some students are really not sure how acquiring another language will benefit them. These students go back and forth between taking an active and passive role. O'Houle (2005) further defines the three approaches that students take to language learning:

Approaches to Language Learning

1. *Activity-oriented learners*

   These learners like to practice language in a social context. They use the social contact with others as a learning context to improve their skills. They are risk takers. They are not afraid to make mistakes. They continually initiate conversations as language practice opportunities.

   > *Activity-oriented learners like to practice language in a social context. They use the social contact with others as a learning context to improve their skills.*

2. *Passive learners*

   These learners remain aloof to language learning. They take awhile to interact with others in conversation. They listen to others rather than interact. They are afraid of making mistakes. They tend to be perfectionists rather than risk takers.

3. *Crossover learners*

   These learners switch between taking active and passive roles. They are more motivated than active or passive learners to use the second language to meet their learning goals. They join others in conversation to meet the goal of finding out information. They don't participate in conversations that don't benefit them in any way (O'Houle, 2005).

   According to O'Houle, Miguel's behavior would indicate that he is an activity-oriented language learner. Maria seems best described as a passive learner. The approach students choose for language learning affects the extent to which they make use of practice opportunities to learn English in the classroom and in social and academic settings.

English Language Learning and Making Use of Practice Opportunities

Practice opportunities are defined as those activities both within and outside the classroom which expose learners to the English language. English learners are differentially motivated to make use of practice opportunities by interacting with target language speakers. Linguists comment on this fact by stating that how students learn a second language is largely dependent on the inner feelings of the learners themselves. They suggest it is not enough to focus on the opportunity itself. It is also important to understand how learners make use of social and academic situations to develop their linguistic competence. It follows that the more students practice, the better their competence should become. English learners who are motivated to actively interact in the second language learn at a faster rate than those who are passive (Fillmore, 2000).

> *English learners who are motivated to actively interact in the second language learn at a faster rate than those who are passive.*

The degree to which English learners are motivated to become actively involved in potential second language practice situations reflects their individual differences including egocentric, attitudinal and social factors. These individual differences reflect the reality that language learning is a highly personal activity that is greatly influenced by students' motivational styles.

Motivational styles are defined as interaction preferences. These adopted communicative patterns may facilitate or impede language learning. Students have the cognitive ability to learn English as a second language. However, the speed at which the language is acquired is closely related to how they utilize practice opportunities. Whether students choose to become passive or active language learners is related to their motivational styles, and reflects their cultural identities.

For many English learners, the sociocultural context of the home and the neighborhood is very different from that of the mainstream sociocultural context of the school. The difference is greater in some families than in others. When the school milieu is very different from the home environment both linguistically and culturally, English learners experience what has been termed

a "psychosocial identity crisis." This is characterized by a sense of confusion, alienation, and discomfort. English learners feel confused by a language that they don't understand. They feel alienated by native English speakers who may initially reject socializing attempts and exclude them from their in-group. Thus, these students who have previously felt very much a part of a family and neighborhood group suddenly feel like outsiders who don't belong.

In addition, English learners experience discomfort in having to relate to new values and traditions which they may interpret as undermining family values. For example, students learning English as a second language may come from families who place great value on group interaction. The school may reflect, conversely, a culture that rewards individual initiative. English learners may feel under pressure to conform so that they may become part of the school culture.

HOME

SCHOOL

Learning a New Language and Culture

Conformity entails taking on not only a new language but a new culture and value system. English learners are faced with having to functionally adapt to two sets of environments, the home and the school settings. They may feel overwhelmed and disoriented when there is little overlap between the two settings. In an attempt to maintain continuity and preserve their personal sense of identity, English learners adapt to the school environment in different ways: by identifying with the school culture and rejecting their home culture, by maintaining their native language identity, or by trying to integrate the two value systems in a bicultural identity. Thus, school entrance becomes a turning point in identity formation for English language learners. Erickson describes this psychological identity crisis "as a necessary turning point, when development must move one way or another" (Erickson, 1990). Students can either marshal resources for growth and the further differentiation of identity or maintain and rigidify their present identity. The motivational styles of English learners include a predisposition as to how they choose to identify with the second language and culture.

English learners are faced with having to functionally adapt to two sets of environments, the home and the school. English learners may feel overwhelmed and disoriented when there is little overlap between the two settings.

Motivational Styles of English Language Learners

Three distinct motivational styles reflect students' preferred mode of participation in second language learning. English learners choose a motivational style to resolve their psychosocial identity crisis.

The first motivational style is labeled *Crystallizing*. Students who manifest this style are passive learners. They choose, at first, to maintain their identity with their native language and culture. They learn the language receptively. They listen, rather than speak. The second motivational style is termed *Crossing Over*. Students who adopt this style in effect do crossover to participate actively in the second language and culture. They seek out social interactions in English. They strive to identify with English speakers. Finally there is the motivational style termed *Crisscrossing*. English learners with this style harmoniously identify with both first and second language cultures. These students feel comfortable code switching between languages to interact in different social and academic settings.

Crystallizing as a motivational style reflects the rigidity of the learner. The attitude of students who adopt this pattern is exemplified by Maria in this example.

Three distinct motivational styles reflect the preferred modes of participation in second language learning which English learners choose to adopt. They choose a motivational style to resolve their psychosocial identity crisis.

Mrs. Rosa Contreras is on a field trip with her class. They are visiting a local river park. There is a small bridge that crosses over a river. On either side of the river are beautiful green fields. The class eats their lunch next to the river. After lunch the students are given a baseball and other play equipment to take advantage of the grassy fields. As students gather together, peer groups begin to emerge. Many of the Spanish speakers congregate together.

Some of the English dominant class members decide to play baseball. They grab a baseball and bat and cross over the bridge. Robert, a native English speaker, starts to assemble a baseball team of girls and boys. He sees Miguel and Maria standing by the bridge and motions for them to come over to play. Miguel is anxious to go and play baseball, but Maria isn't. Miguel tries to persuade Maria to go with him. They have the following conversation.

The Crytallizing Motivational Style

Miguel: Maria, C'mon let's go and play baseball.

Maria: No, quiero quedarme aquí con Rosa, Marisol y Carlos.
         (No, I want to stay here with Rosa, Marisol and Carlos.)

Miguel: C'mon, Maria. Let's join the team.

Maria: Prefiero jugar con mis propios amigos.
         No quiero jugar con los otros estudiantes.
         (I'd rather play with my own friends.
         I don't want to play with the other students.)

Miguel: Let's go Maria.

Maria: No, no estoy segura como decir las cosas que quiero en
         inglés.
         (No, I'm not sure how to say the things I want in English.)

Miguel: Ven. Yo puedo ayudarte.
         (Come. I can help you.)

Maria: No, quiero quedarme aquí.
         (No, I want to stay here.)

Miguel: Entonces me voy.
         (Then I'm going.)

         I'm coming over, Robert.

Maria's responses show the high positive value she places on her first language and culture. She construes speaking Spanish as a marker of group membership.

Miguel pleads with Maria to accompany him to play baseball with the English speakers. Maria replies, *"No, quiero quedarme aquí con Rosa, Marisol y Carlos." (No, I want to stay here with Rosa, Marisol and Carlos.)* Maria further explains her statement to Miguel by asserting her preference for playing with her own friends instead of playing with the other students. *"Prefiero jugar con mis propios amigos. No quiero jugar con los otros estudiantes." (I'd rather play with my own friends. I don't want to play with the other students.)* Maria's responses show the high positive value she places on her first language and culture. She construes speaking Spanish as a marker of group membership. The ideological affiliation she has with native language speakers takes precedence over participation in the second language and culture.

Maria's desire is to maintain Spanish as her most frequent language pattern for social interactions. She thus remains a passive English language learner.

The exclusivity that Maria exhibits by clearly stating that she prefers the familiarity of remaining with Spanish language speakers also reflects her attitude toward English speakers. Maria chooses to set herself apart from English-speaking peers. She does not want to socially interact or identify with them. She refuses to cross over and play with the English speakers. Maria thus crystallizes her native language identity by standing firm in her position to remain passive. She doesn't choose to participate in language learning opportunities.

Maria's stance also reflects her personality characteristics. Maria appears to be very self-critical. It is very important to her that she maintain her dignity and pride. She refuses to speak English until she can do so without errors. Maria doesn't like the uncertainty of not being able to express herself in a social interaction with English speakers.

For this reason, she opts to socialize in her native language. She can communicate effectively and easily in Spanish. She doesn't feel confident speaking English. This fact is reflected in Maria's statement to Miguel, *"No estoy segura como decir las cosas que quiero en inglés."* (I'm not sure how to say the things I want in English.) Maria's position not to speak English until she is comfortable remains fixed even after Miguel offers to help her communicate in English, saying, *"Yo puedo ayudarte."* (I can help you). Maria remains adamant. She repeats, *"No, quiero quedarme aquí."* (No, I want to stay here.)

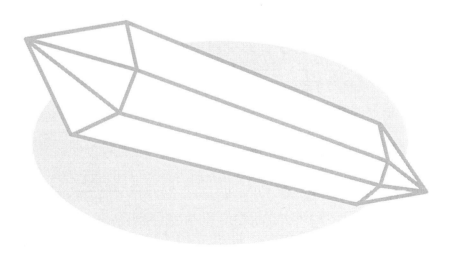

Crystallizers and Passive Language Learning

In the classroom, students who adhere to the *Crystallizing* motivational style are best characterized as passive English language learners. Their behavior may be reactive to input, but they do little to initiate situations which cause more input to be directed at them. These students tend to interact inside and outside the classroom primarily with others who speak their mother tongue. They communicate with the teacher in English only when prodded during structured lessons. As passive learners they do not seek out practice opportunities, but instead retreat and avoid interacting with English speakers. These students are therefore highly dependent on classroom activities which structure discourse for practicing academic language.

> **In the classroom, students who adhere to the Crystallizing motivational style are best characterized as passive English learners.**

Mrs. Rosa Contreras understands Maria's Crystallizing motivational style causes her to remain on the sidelines. Maria chooses not to express herself in academic settings. Mrs. Contreras, therefore, arranges structured academic language learning opportunities. She pairs Maria with an English speaker for assignments that require communicative interaction.

Linguists label students like Maria who adopt a *Crystallizing* motivational style as "low input generators." Low input generators are described as: receiving a limited amount of focused input in the English language, not seeking out practice opportunities, and as displaying avoidance behaviors toward English language speakers. *Crystallizers*, as low input generators, are not motivated to take advantage of communicative encounters. They instead sit quietly on the periphery of the group, contributing little to English discussion unless specifically asked by the teacher to do so.

Crystallizers approach language learning slowly and cautiously. Expressive English language usage is restricted to those statements which they can make confidently without error. Spontaneous verbalization in English is obviously missing. In large groups these students rarely volunteer answers. When they do respond to a directed question, *Crystallizers* appear to be analyzing or translating before speaking. They sometimes repeat words they hear very softly, often in tones inaudible to a person more than a few feet away. Utterances are typically shorter than other students' responses.

The emphasis in second-language learning is clearly placed by *Crystallizers* on receptive understanding. They engage in long periods of silent observation until the language code is absorbed. Perfection in comprehension is expected before a commitment is made to verbalization.

Mr. Edward Marcos teaches eighth grade. Half his students are English language learners. He has a number of students that he recognizes as having a Crystallizing motivational style. Mr. Marcos is aware that these students use successive approximation techniques for mastering the English language. These include four sequential steps: 1) receptive understanding of the language 2) sequential testing of individual words 3) use of language in paired lesson related activities and finally, 4) verbalization for social and academic interactions.

Mr. Marcos makes use of these successive approximation techniques. He gives Crystallizers lots of opportunities to gain a receptive understanding of the language before he requires them to speak. He initially has students point to words to match pictures. He uses yes and no response cards that students can hold up for answers. As students feel more comfortable with the English language, he encourages them to respond to questions using words and short phrases. He structures vocabulary building activities around paired learning. He pairs Crystallizers with native English speakers. He does not force students to engage in group activities until they are ready and confident.

The emphasis in second language learning is clearly placed by Crystallizers on receptive understanding.

Crystallizers express themselves socially and academically in the English language as the final step of language learning. This is the result of their persistence in code switching to the native language. This may be due to an insecurity and unfamiliarity with both the English language and culture. This causes them to fear interacting with those whom they don't know intimately or socially. When *Crystallizers* do begin speaking to English peers they initially attend to how well their speech is being received and whether their performance meets with learned receptive standards.

The motivational style of *Crystallizing* can be summed up as a passive attitude toward English learning. Students with this motivational style have personality characteristics that predispose them to hold back from speaking the language

until they are totally confident. Cornejo notes, "learners who are cautious in their attitudes toward the second language may initially be less successful" (Cornejo, 2006). Learning is blocked for these students because of their tendency to avoid situations in which they must communicate in English. They resist speaking English because it will force them to change their usual style of communication, a style that is extremely familiar and comfortable to them. They react to the psychosocial identity crisis by tenaciously holding onto and crystallizing their first language identity.

The Crossing Over Motivational Style

The motivational style of Crystallizing can be summed up as a passive attitude toward English language learning. Students with this motivational style have personality characteristics that predispose them to hold back from speaking the language until they are totally confident.

In direct contrast to *Crystallizers* are English language learners whose motivational style can be termed *Crossing Over*. Students with this style choose to actively pursue the learning of English. Many even totally give up speaking the native language in the school setting. These students actively elicit stimulation and response from native English speakers. They engage in dynamic interactions. By initiating and engaging in academic conversations with English language speakers, these students experience a reflexive response in the form of more language input to themselves.

The motivational style, *Crossing Over*, describes those students who make a deliberate effort to get English speakers to interact with them. They seem to intuitively sense that they are dependent on native speakers to provide them with appropriate models. These students don't sit and wait to be addressed but rather seek out English speakers. *Crossovers* capitalize on English practice opportunities both in and out of the classroom. They are less dependent on language learning from structured drills. They rely on academic conversational contexts for learning language. *Crossovers* are motivated to continually pick up chunks of language from conversations and imitate these chunks in formal and informal school settings.

Mr. James Langford is a high school teacher. He has a number of English learners with the Crossover motivational style. He knows these students are motivated to learn language through social interactions. He, therefore, arranges cooperative group activities mixing English learners with native English speakers. He assigns activities that require students to use the functions of language which include: giving information, asking questions, giving commands and using language to create solutions to problems. Mr. Langford continually uses cooperative group activities as follow up to direct instruction. He takes advantage of the proclivity of Crossovers to learn language from their English speaking peers.

The term *Crossing Over* symbolizes the attitude of students toward mastering the English language. Students who choose this participant structure of interaction project a positive attitude, an admiration, and warmth toward English speakers. They are not so emotionally committed to their first language that they are unwilling to accommodate to the new language and culture. These students believe that communication serves many cognitive and social functions in the school setting.

Crossovers often detach themselves temporarily from native language peers. They choose to address the psychosocial identity crisis by initially crossing over to identify with the second language and culture in the school setting.

The high value placed on becoming bilingual is made apparent by the overriding desire of *Crossovers* to identify with English language speakers. *Crossovers* often detach themselves, temporarily from native language peers. They choose to address the psychosocial identity crisis by initially crossing over to identify with the second language and culture in the school setting.

Crossing Over and Active Language Learning

Personality variables of the Crossing Over motivational style include: flexibility, impulsiveness, and a sense of independence. Flexibility is noted as *Crossovers* assimilate English as a second language into their current existing psychological structures. They modify these structures by accommodating to the demands of the new environment (Laosa, 2005). English learners with the *Crossing Over* style view identification with English speakers as necessary for their successful adaptation to the school environment. Impulsivity is expressed by *Crossovers'* willingness to take chances. They jump right into a series of social and academic encounters without analyzing the situations or their competence to interact in English. They remain unflustered even when they have difficulty expressing themselves. A sense of independence is revealed by these students' self-assertiveness. From the beginning stages of English language learning, *Crossovers* adopt an attitude of personal responsibility. They appear uninhibited. They display a relaxed and open attitude to the language learning experience.

> *From the beginning stages of English language learning, Crossovers adopt an attitude of personal responsibility. They appear uninhibited. They display a relaxed and open attitude to the language learning experience.*

Miguel is characterized as having the Crossing Over motivational style. He is anxious to play with the English speakers. He does not remain with Maria when she refuses to cross over. He expresses an independence in his statement, "Entonces, me voy." (Then, I'm going.) He does not want to hang back. He wants to venture out into the English speaking community. He crosses over to join the English speakers with a sense of confidence. By doing this, he cuts himself temporarily adrift from his native language peers.

Students with the *Crossing Over* motivational style often distance themselves from native language speakers temporarily. They do this to advance their communicative competence in the English language. It is as if they feel immersion in the second language is the most expedient way to develop English proficiency. They *cross over* to establish immediate social ties with English speakers. The abrupt and active transfer from speaking the native language to English distinguishes the *Crossing Over* motivational style from the *Crystallizing* style which is marked by gradual change and passive learning.

The Crisscrossing Motivational Style

The third motivational style is termed *Crisscrossing*. English language learners who choose this participant structure habitually switch between two languages and cultures. They often verbalize by mixing the two languages. Cornejo describes this mixing as the use of grammatical, lexical, and phonological aspects of both English and Spanish within single sentences (Cornejo, 2006). The mixing of English and Spanish is manifested in communication patterns which include code-switching in different cultural settings. *Crisscrossers* interact with both native language and English speakers. No preference is shown for one group over the other. Unlike *Crystallizers*, they do not cling exclusively to their native language; neither do they, like *Crossovers*, abandon their native language for a time in favor of English.

   Crisscrossers have a positive attitude toward both the first and second language and hence teeter-totter between the two. They seem to want to integrate a wide range of experience into their social and academic language repertoire by interacting with both cultural groups. They try to maintain a balance between the two languages.

CRISSCROSS

The third motivational style is termed Crisscrossing. English language learners who choose this participant structure habitually switch between two languages and cultures. They often verbalize by mixing the two languages.

Crisscrossers and Code Switching

Crisscrossers are constantly comparing and contrasting communicative phrases in social and academic conversations. When *Crisscrossers* have difficulty expressing themselves in one language, they borrow from the other one. Even though *Crisscrossers* are comfortable integrating words from both languages in their communication, they don't approach the learning of the English language as intensely as *Crossovers*. On the other hand, they do not take the passive attitude of *Crystallizers*. They outpace these students in initial expressive language use.

Crisscrossers react to the psychosocial identity crisis by formulating a bicultural identity. Crisscrossers don't give up their native language or culture but instead maintain it and adopt an English language identity as well.

Crisscrossers' personality variables include versatility, adaptability, and spontaneity. Versatility is expressed in *Crisscrossers'* ability to easily code switch back and forth between languages. Students with this style transfer language and culture mannerisms from one culture to the other. Their adaptability is noted in their verbal interactions. *Crisscrossers* appear to feel comfortable in new situations and adjust their communication patterns appropriately.

The flow of conversation is of primary importance to *Crisscrossers*. This communication flow is maintained by the inserting of a first language word for an unknown label in English. Translation is another important communication strategy used by *Crisscrossers*. They often rely on bilinguals to translate their messages for English speaking peers. The spontaneity of *Crisscrossers* is revealed in the quickness of their responses. Their quick spontaneous responses in English, however, sometimes suffer from incoherency. The poor sequential arrangement of borrowed words from both languages often contributes to this incoherence.

Crisscrossers react to the psychosocial identity crisis by formulating a bicultural identity. *Crisscrossers* don't give up their native language or culture but instead maintain it and adopt an English language identity as well. They switch back and forth between identities. They settle ultimately on cultural consolidation and accommodation as an approach to learning English as a second language.

The degree to which English language learners identify with native English speakers may be thought of as positions along a motivation continuum. The identification with English speaking peers involves a process of simultaneous reflection and observation, a process taking place on all levels of mental and emotional functioning. English learners choose the way and degree in which they will identify or not identify with the English language and culture. This choice is influenced by their attitudes, emotions, personality characteristics and motivational styles.

English learners choose different ways to resolve the identity crisis which results from discontinuities between cultures. Students who choose to initially reject their first language and culture in favor of identifying with English speakers have the *Crossing Over* motivational style. Students who choose to maintain their first language identify reveal a *Crystallizing* style. Finally, those students who quickly develop a bicultural identity and equally balance the two cultures manifest the *Crisscrossing* style.

Students' motivational styles determine whether the language is approached with tremor or bravado. It is important to note that no one style is better than another. Students with all three styles learn English eventually. Motivational styles, however, clarify the personality and attitudinal characteristics which permit some English language learners to progress more quickly than others.

The Best Practice teacher needs to understand how students differ in their approaches to language learning so he or she can plan and differentiate activities. Instruction in this way can fit the personalities and feelings of learners rather than a programmed text.

While the differentiation of instruction for motivational styles is important, all English learners benefit from being grouped with proficient English speakers. Crystallizers benefit from hearing the English language spoken in the context of a content activity. Crossovers revile in the conversations that they can have with their English-speaking peers. Crisscrossers are content to move back and forth between languages constantly inserting the new vocabulary they learn.

> *English learners choose the way and degree in which they will identify or not identify with the English language and culture. This choice is influenced by their attitudes, emotions, personality characteristics and motivational styles.*

The *Best Practice* teacher provides differentiated English language learning opportunities for students. Activities are designed by the teacher to give students control over how fast and through what approach they will master English as a second language.

Language learning is facilitated for all motivational styles through the use of academic and social conversations. The teacher structures the school day to permit time for dialogue. Conversations between the teacher and English language learners should be unstructured and flow naturally from the social encounter. The following conversation between a first grade English language learner and the teacher is an example of natural communication.

> Teacher: *That bunny you're drawing is very fat.*
>
> Student: *It's a mommy bunny. All mommy bunnies are fat.*
>
> Teacher: *Well, maybe she should go on a diet.*
>
> Student: *Yeah, my mommy's got a diet. She eats only…you know.*
>
> Teacher: *I should go on a diet too, but I like cookies too much.*
>
> Student: *You like cookies! Me too! Chocolate chip — big ones!*

The teacher structures the school day to permit time for dialogue. Conversations between the teacher and English language learners should be unstructured and flow naturally from the social encounter.

This conversation between the student and teacher flows in the form of a social dialogue. The teacher builds on the student's statements. A sense of rapport develops between the teacher and student as they share their love of cookies. The student expresses her amazement that the teacher actually likes cookies. (You like cookies!) Often teachers don't realize that students, especially young students, don't see them as real human beings with needs and wants just as they have. Conversations are the building blocks that lead to the identification between students and the teacher. By building on social dialogue, the teacher allows students to perceive him or her as a fellow human being with whom they can identify.

Dialogue and The Flow of Meaning

The Best Practice teacher keeping in mind that dialogue means "flow of meaning" uses conversations to facilitate English language learning for middle school and high school students.

Teacher: *What's your favorite sport?*

Student: *I like soccer.*

Teacher: *I like soccer too. Did you watch the World Cup between France and Italy?*

Student: *Yes, I like the game.*

Teacher: *You liked the game. I liked the game too. I especially liked it when Italy made the last goal and won the game.*

The Best Practice teacher keeping in mind that dialogue means "flow of meaning" uses conversations to facilitate English language learning for middle school and high school students.

Notice in this example that the teacher did not correct the student when he used the present rather than the past tense. (Yes, I like the game.) This would have destroyed the intimacy of the encounter. Rather, she just modeled the correct tense in her succeeding statements.

As the teacher has social conversations with English language learners, he or she will become more acutely aware that students respond according to their personality and motivational style. *Crystallizers* may initially be very reticent, replying in monosyllables. *Crossovers* will chatter on and on, loving the social encounter.

Crisscrossers will verbalize in sentences that will include words from both languages. They will often ask the teacher for the translation of native language words. Regardless of how students initially respond to the teacher, he or she can be sure that English language learners have benefited in their own unique way from the social encounter.

The acceptance of students as individuals with unique personalities that influence their language learning can be further addressed by the Best Practice teacher through the harmonious matching of motivational style with instructional strategies. Students with the *Crystallizing* motivational style respond at first best to listening activities including computer-assisted learning. Computer-assisted receptive learning activities give *Crystallizers* the opportunity to gain a listening comprehension of the language before oral production. As *Crystallizers* begin to produce language, they can best be encouraged through communicative activities that stress choral response. These activities allow *Crystallizers* to participate as part of a group.

Successful adaptation to the school environment is impeded if it is different in critical ways from that of the home.

The academic use of language can be stimulated through the "buddy system." This method pairs *Crystallizers* with English language speakers for structured and unstructured content-based activities. The success of this technique depends on the teacher's perceptiveness in arranging congenial pairs. *Crystallizers* should be paired with English speakers who take an active interest in others, even a "mothering" approach, rather than an overly aggressive stance.

Crystallizers are usually at war with themselves as they try to establish some continuity between the home and school milieus. Successful adaptation to the school environment is impeded if it is different in critical ways from that of the home. In the face of real discontinuities, *Crystallizers* may give up trying and rigidify in their first language identity. Upper grade students who find it difficult to adapt to the English speaking environment may become so discouraged that they drop out of school.

Best Practice Teaching for Motivational Styles

The *Best Practice* teacher helps *Crystallizers* adjust to the second language and culture by examining those aspects of the school environment that are most discontinuous with the home. Once these elements have been noted, the teacher establishes communication patterns that promote two-way understandings between cultures. Intercultural communication is facilitated by the teacher who makes a concentrated effort to understand how English correlates with home language variables such as: content and tone, cultural patterns, aspirations and values. Too often the cultural values of students are just as foreign to teachers as the second language and culture is to students.

It is important to remember that *Crystallizers* go through what is termed "a silent period" during which they listen and observe more than they speak. *Crystallizers* are uncomfortable speaking until their grammar and their experience with English word order is solidified. They also may be afraid of being ridiculed for using "accented" English speech reflecting their inexperience with English sounds and stress patterns.

Although *Crystallizers* are quiet in class, they are hard at work listening and comprehending. They learn language gradually. The teacher can facilitate learning for these students by not exerting pressure on them to speak before they are ready. Providing content activities that allow *Crystallizers* to receptively learn content and critical academic vocabulary, gives these students the foundation they need to feel comfortable with the new communication system.

The teacher encourages English language learners with the *Crossing Over* motivational style by arranging cooperative group activities. *Crossovers* learn the second language naturally when they are given freedom and the opportunity to interact with English speakers. *Crossovers* should be exposed to a combination of structured and unstructured group activities. Structured activities include: completing content practice assignments, research internet projects, prediction mind maps, graphic organizers and problem solving activities. Unstructured activities include team sports, music groups, drama groups or other school activities where language flows from the social context.

Crossovers, who are highly motivated to identify with English speakers, greatly benefit from exposure to a variety of language models. Learning English from a diversified selection of peers and the teacher permits students to acquire a broader range of social expressions, idioms and academic vocabulary. By arranging peer and group assignments, the teacher helps students develop the academic and social language patterns they need to be successful in school across subject areas.

> **Students with the Crossing Over motivational style need to be involved in structuring some of their academic learning experiences. Crossovers seem to intuitively know how to create opportunities that facilitate their learning of academic vocabulary.**

Students with the *Crossing Over* motivational style need to be involved in structuring some of their academic learning experiences. *Crossovers* seem to intuitively know how to create opportunities that facilitate their learning of academic vocabulary. They use inner guides to direct them to focus on words that have the most transfer value across the curriculum. *Crossovers* naturally see patterns and make connections from one subject discipline to another.

The teacher can facilitate learning of academic language for these students through a thematic approach to learning. The targeting of tier two interdisciplinary words for instruction accelerates students' ability to comprehend subject area texts. It also gives *Crossovers* the basis for written communication.

The *Best Practice* teacher facilitates learning for students with the *Crisscrossing* motivational style by helping these students separate the native language and English as two distinct language systems. *Crisscrossers* find language learning easier when they are made aware of the linguistic similarities and differences which exist at the functional, as well as the structural level. Awareness develops as the teacher gives feedback to students in structured and unstructured situations on the correct linking of vocabulary and grammatical configurations. Similar grammatical patterns that overlap languages need to be stressed in Spanish. This enables students to apply rules from a single grammatical pool. Likewise, the teaching of cognates is

important for *Crisscrossers*. These students will immediately begin to apply English words that look like and have similar meanings to the words they already know in Spanish.

The learning of Spanish-English cognates also helps *Crisscrossers* immediately comprehend words in the context of a reading. Words like generosity (generosidad) and gesture (gesto) are easily deciphered and understood.

Instructional focus for *Crisscrossers* should center on functional communication in each language that does not depend on language mixing. Clear separation of languages by time, location, or speaker dissuades *Crisscrossers* from communicating with fragments from both languages. It also strengthens their ability to use each linguistic system holistically.

Languages can be kept distinct for *Crisscrossers* through a 50-50 dual immersion model in which the native language is taught for half the day and English is taught for the other half. Current brain research supports the concept of dual language immersion. Studies have shown that students develop another part of the brain when they are instructed equally in two languages (Zadina, 2007). Cognitive development is promoted through structured content learning in both languages. The integrity of both languages are maintained through an additive approach.

The discussion of motivational styles is meant to give teachers insights into approaches for differentiating instruction for English learners. Although the examples given target only Spanish speakers, the motivational styles apply to English language learners from all language groups.

> **Studies have shown that students develop another part of the brain when they are instructed equally in two languages.**

By becoming sensitive to the different ways students approach language learning, the teacher can more easily modify subject delivery. The teacher can also answer a strategic question such as, *Is English language learning blocked for students by internal fears or does the difficulty result from the method of presentation?*

While some English language learners may thrive on one instructional approach, others may struggle. By effectively using differentiated instructional activities, the teacher creates learning situations through which students can acquire English most comfortably and easily.

Differentiated learning activities matched to motivational styles include:

Computer-Assisted Listening Activities – *(Crystallizers)*

The use of bilingual texts.

Cooperative Group Activities – *(Crossovers)*

Vocabulary Activities – divided in two sections by language *(Crisscrossers)*

The English Language Development Standards Framework for California Public Schools for grades kindergarten through high school acknowledges the importance of addressing different learning styles. It states:

The Framework is based on the assumption that all students will attain proficiency in English, but the framework also recognizes that all learners will not acquire skills and knowledge at the same rate or in the same way. The needs of English learners are addressed in the standards by providing different pathways for students that address learning styles and critical developmental differences for students who enter school at various grade levels (English Language Development Standards for California Public School, 2002).

> **Learning how to facilitate English language development becomes critical considering that more than 40% of the students in California speak a language other than English. These percentages are matched in many other states.**

Learning how to facilitate English language development becomes critical considering that more than 40% of the students in California speak a language other than English. These percentages are matched in many other states. Since English learners enter school at all grade levels, high school teachers as well as elementary teachers must learn effective teaching strategies. One strategy that can be used across grade levels is interdisciplinary teaching that ties subject specific tier 3 words and interdisciplinary tier 2 words to content concepts.

Mrs. Cardiff is teaching world history. The topic or theme she chooses for the class is World Changing Innovations. Her goal is to have students use both textual and digital resources to answer the Strategic Question: *What is the greatest innovation of the last 150 years?* Mrs. Cardiff directs students to research the topic from multiple sources and perspectives. She provides a list of important interdisciplinary tier two words and useful expressions for English learners who range from early production to fluent speakers.

World Changing Innovations

- the invention of the telephone
- the discovery of penicillin
- the invention of the car
- the exploration of space
- the development of rap music
- the invention of the microchip
- the spread of democracy through the world

Useful Interdisciplinary Words

- *achieve*
- *break*
- *make*
- *worthwhile*
- *create*
- *achievement*
- *important*
- *argument*
- *invention*
- *changed*
- *result*

Useful Phrases

- *the invention or discovery has led to...*
- *it is of great importance because*
- *has completely changed people's lives because...*
- *as a result people in the world have been able to...*

Students can choose to answer the Strategic Question by giving a short oral presentation, or through a written report. Students can elect to work individually, in pairs or in a group. Mrs. Cardiff has found YouTube sites and Internet links where students can listen to explanations of how each innovation changed the world. Students take notes and formulate their own questions as they actively listen. Bilingual links and texts are used by English learners to acquire the information they need to answer the question.

At the end of the unit students compare their answers with their peers. Mrs. Cardiff extends students' learning by posing open-ended questions such as *Do you agree or disagree with_____? What do you think will be the most important innovation in the next hundred years? How can you become part of an innovative team?* English learners and all students benefit from the vocabulary and higher level thinking that is applied in the thematic lesson.

Considering students' motivational styles in planning classroom activities accelerates students' learning. Research shows that students adopt the use of language patterns at an early age. Unique personality variables lead students to choose a particular style and this choice affects initial English language learning. The teacher by understanding the affective domain of language learning can design classroom activities that ensure the success of all students.

Think About Discussion Questions

1. Use the following chart to analyze three factors that affect the motivation of English language learners. Give a classroom example relating to the subject or subjects you teach.

Motivational Factor	How does it affect language learning?	Classroom Example

2. Review the English Development Standards for students at your grade level. Evaluate and write a reflection on one Internet Web site that provides standards-based language development for English learners at the grade level or in the subject area you teach.

Reflection on Motivational Styles of English Language Learners

1. Reflect on your own experience learning a second or foreign language. How would you analyze your motivational style of language learning? Evaluate how your motivational style facilitated or impeded the learning of the foreign language.

    (If you have never learned a foreign language in school, hypothesize what your style would be).

2. Reflect on the English Language Development Standards for your grade level. Create an activity to teach one of the standards in the context of a subject other than language arts. The activity should address your students' language proficiency levels

Chapter 4

Linking Teacher Support and Active Learning

A research study examined middle school students perceptions of the conditions that fostered their meaningful engagement in classroom learning.

*Middle school students were asked:
What kind of activity engages you in learning?*

*Middle school students responded:
Instructional activities that are meaningful, varied and interesting and involve group learning.*

*Middle school students were asked:
What kinds of activities disengage you in learning?*

*Middle school students responded:
Rote learning, routines and long periods of direct instruction.*

Student Engagement and Achievement

- *Is there a connection between high motivation and student engagement in learning?*

- *Does student engagement in learning contribute to academic achievement?*

- *How do researchers define student engagement?*

- *Why do students become less engaged as they grow older?*

- *What kinds of learning environments promote student engagement and achievement?*

- *How is teacher support linked to student engagement and achievement?*

> *There is a consensus among researchers and reformers that high student motivation and engagement in learning has a significant correlation to academic achievement in school regardless of socioeconomic status.*

As the pressure mounts from high stakes standards-based testing and high school exit exams, increasingly researchers and school reformers have focused on Best Practices for increasing student achievement. There is a consensus among researchers and reformers that high student motivation and engagement in learning has a significant correlation to academic achievement in school regardless of socioeconomic status (Klem, 2004).

Highly motivated and engaged students are more likely to earn higher grades and score at the proficient or advanced levels on high-stakes testing. They also have lower drop out rates. In contrast, students with low levels of motivation and engagement get lower grades, score at lower levels on high stakes testing and are more likely to drop out of school. The National Center for Educational Statistics notes that disengaged students have higher levels of absenteeism and a lower participation rate in school activities. This leads eventually to their high drop out rates.

Research studies further show that the longer students attend school the more disengaged they become. Patterns of disengagement with school including boredom, off task behavior and lack of interest begin as early as third grade. Disengagement increases from third grade to middle school to high school (Croninger, 2004). By high school as many as 40-60% of students become chronically disengaged.

Contrary to popular belief, disengaged students are not just struggling learners. They are also academically gifted students who do not find schooling relevant or interesting. This is especially true as the divide increases between a technologically driven 21st century world with change at its core and the often static, bureaucratic and traditional school structures.

Students, who are bombarded with interactive visual and auditory stimuli in their daily 21st century living, often find it difficult to adjust to hours of passive direct instruction. Yet, schooling is just as essential for students who will spend their lives in the 21st century as it was for those raised in the industrial age. Students need research and communication skills to sort through myriads of 21st century facts. They need to understand how these facts relate to each other through interdisciplinary learning. The question is not whether students need schooling. The question that remains elusive is how best to engage students in meaningful and relevant learning.

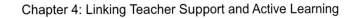

Engaging Students in Learning

In an effort to answer the question of how best to engage students in learning, researchers have approached the challenge from a number of perspectives. These include: a theoretical perspective, a cause-and-consequence perspective and a *Best Practice* perspective.

Marks studied "engagement" from a theoretical perspective. She proposed a definition of engagement that would help operationalize and explain the concept.

Marks defined engagement as a psychological process. Specifically, it is students' attention, interest and investment directed toward learning (Marks, 2001). Students' attention is defined as their mastery of the knowledge, skills and crafts associated with academic work. Students' interest is assessed in relation to their emotional involvement and commitment to learning at school. Their investment is related to how strongly they are motivated to overcome challenges to succeed at school.

Students' engagement in learning was considered by Marks as a positive psychological attitude (Marks, 2001). According to this perspective, positive attitudinal changes lead to students' engagement in learning.

The cause-and-consequence perspective was defined by Connell as: "ongoing engagement and reaction to challenge." Ongoing engagement was associated with students' behaviors during the school day including: time spent on task, intensity of concentration and emotional commitment to learning. Reaction to challenge was defined in relation to students' coping strategies for dealing with a challenge. Connell noted that students coped with learning challenges by either trying harder or by giving up and withdrawing (Connell, 2004).

According to the cause-and-consequence perspective students become engaged in learning through the teacher's reinforcement of their coping mechanisms. These include: increased effort, strategic thinking, problem solving, information seeking and experimentation. Positive coping mechanisms cause a chain of events that allow students to meet learning challenges successfully.

> *Ongoing engagement was associated with students' behaviors during the school day including: time spent on task, intensity of concentration and emotional commitment to learning.*

The *Best Practice* perspective addresses the challenge of how to engage students in learning through teacher support, active versus passive learning and student engagement strategies and techniques. Teacher support has been linked to student engagement in several studies. The research manifests that students who have more caring and supportive interpersonal relationships with their teachers report positive attitudes toward schooling and more active engagement in learning (Patrick, 2007).

Teacher Support and Student Engagement

A research study guided by the Self System Process Model developed by Connell (see Chart A) explains students' engagement by examining linkages between teacher support, student engagement and student achievement. Linkages are explored and examined in the study along with two research questions: 1) *What levels of teacher support are critical for students' engagement and academic success?* and 2) *How much difference does achieving the threshold levels contribute to the likelihood of high academic achievement?* (Connell, 2004)

> *The research manifests that students who have more caring and supportive interpersonal relationships with their teachers report positive attitudes toward schooling and more active engagement in learning.*

Chart A
The Reduced Self System Process Model (adapted from Connell, 2004)

Teacher Support		
School Context	**Action**	**Outcomes**
Reinforcement of on task behavior →	Student Engagement →	Accelerated Performance
Reinforcement of positive reactions to challenges →	Student Engagement →	Academic Achievement
Techniques that involve students in learning →	Student Engagement →	School Attendance

The results of this study of over 5,000 students from elementary to high school revealed that teacher support is critical to student engagement and achievement.

Students were highly engaged when they perceived teachers as creating a caring and well-organized learning environment. The environment included clear expectations and a balance of group, individual and creative construction activities. Students' engagement was associated with increased attendance and higher test scores. Links between teacher support, students' engagement and academic performance were noted across grade levels.

The effects of teacher support and students' engagement in learning were greater at the middle school than elementary level. Whereas 48% of elementary school students became more engaged when they experienced teacher support, 75% of middle school students became more engaged. The increased involvement of middle school students resulted in greater school success (Connell, 2004).

Supportive teachers challenge students by teaching them: strategic thinking, linear and nonlinear Web-based research skills and right brain creative, possibility thinking.

Researchers noted that higher levels of teacher support correlated with higher levels of students' motivation. Rather than identifying critical levels for support, studies showed the more support the better. The question of how much difference teacher support made in terms of students' school success was answered by statistics. It was clear that middle school students were motivated even more than elementary students by teacher support. Whereas, 68% of highly engaged elementary students showed higher academic performance, 75% of middle school students manifested increased achievement (Connell, 2004).

Connell concluded from the increased achievement manifested by engaged learners that teachers need to create more personalized and challenging learning environments. Supportive teachers challenge students by teaching them: strategic thinking, linear and nonlinear Web-based research skills, and right brain creative possibility thinking. Most importantly, teachers challenge students by giving them responsibility for their own learning. The ultimate payoff for the teacher who effectively engages students in the learning process is the high level of academic performance of his or her students across subject areas and on high stakes testing.

The Best Practice perspective on student engagement requires the facilitation of students' learning in an active learning environment. Active learning implies that learners are given choices on how to acquire knowledge. The teacher facilitates this process by designing learning activities based on Gardner's eight intelligences.

Students are given learning tasks that encourage them to use one or several modalities to apply and demonstrate their learning. They are encouraged by the teacher to make their own decisions on how to use facts and concepts to express their understandings. The teacher helps students make connections to what they are learning. She or he helps students understand why what they are learning is important to their futures (Jablon, 2006).

Students who participate in an active learning environment become intrinsically motivated learners. Active learners can be considered the antithesis of disengaged learners. These are the students who can't wait for the dismissal bell everyday. They see no purpose in learning as they sit in rows and listen to hour after hour of direct instruction accompanied by factual questions. They rarely participate in learning because they know that no matter what they think about a topic, there is only one correct answer. They are not motivated by assignments that must be completed in just one way. As the year progresses, these disengaged learners become chronically absent and eventually give up coming to school at all by dropping out.

Active Learning and Student Engagement

Engaged students unlike disengaged students are active participants in the learning process. They chorally respond to open-ended questions. They use physical responses or response cards. They share their ideas with a partner. They interact in group problem solving. This kind of active learning environment can be created through *Best Practice* student engagement strategies that:

- *involve students in the learning process;*

- *focus students on learning important skills and content understandings;*

- *support constructivism or learning by doing;*

- *foster 21ˢᵗ century learning paradigms;*

- *support students in using electronic media; and*

- *encourage creative problem solving and applied imagination.*

> *Engaged students unlike disengaged students are active participants in the learning process. They chorally respond to open-ended questions. They use physical responses or response cards. They share their ideas with a partner.*

Best Practice student engagement strategies first and foremost involve students in the learning process through physical responses including: hand signals, changing physical positions, choral answers and response cards. Hand responses are like choral responses. All students are involved and engaged. Instead of one student answering the teacher's question by raising his or her hand, all students in the class put their thumbs up to answer the question as yes and thumbs down to answer the question as no. A thumb to the side means the student does not know. Other hand signals include shaking the hand up and down for yes and sideways for no.

Physical responses including hand signals encourage students' active participation in learning. The teacher may ask students who agree with a statement to stand up, wave their hands or put their hands on their heads. Students together can give choral responses or paired responses.

Recent brain research supports the use of physical responses for student engagement and their retention of information. Activity, according to brain research, sends more glucose to the brain and increases learning.

Recent brain research supports the use of physical responses for student engagement and their retention of information. Activity, according to brain research, sends more glucose to the brain and increases learning (Zadina, 2007). Physical responses like standing up and giving choral responses actively involve students in learning and mastering the content standards.

A movie classic, *Stand Up and Deliver,* documents the physical responses that the teacher, Jaime Escalante, used to motivate East Los Angeles high school students to successfully pass an advanced placement calculus exam.

After establishing a positive belief system by telling the Latino students that they have a history of greatness, Escalante set out to actively change apathetic learners into enthusiastic students. He squelched any apathy by getting students involved in learning. He continually had students give choral responses. He had students actually do what the movie says *stand up and deliver* the math formulas as seen in this example:

Everyone stand up against the wall like a snake. You are the best. You have math in your blood. It was your ancestors, the Mayans that came up with the concept of zero.

Now everyone tell me the formula. A negative times a negative equals a positive. Everyone, say it. Say it again. This time say it louder. Tell the person next to you the formula. A negative times a negative equals a positive.

Another educator featured in the movie, Mr. Holland's Opus, when given the challenge of teaching music to a football player, did not begin the learning process by having him read sheet music. Instead, Mr. Holland actively engaged the student in learning the beat to music by dancing it, clapping it and beating the rhythm on his desk.

Mr. Holland even went so far as to put a football helmet on the student's head. Then he tapped out the beat. Needless to say, the football player did get the beat.

Physical responses are powerful student engagement strategies that the Best Practice teacher uses to engage students in learning any subject area. Academic vocabulary can be successfully taught not only in core subject areas but also in Physical Education and in elective courses.

Mr. Ken Adams is actively engaging his eighth grade basketball class in learning multiple meaning tier two vocabulary words using the Rule of 3. As the teacher models a lay-up, he introduces the terms: dribble, bank, backboard, net, basket, run, pass and field goal. He has students use the terms while they are practicing lay-ups. After the drill, he discusses the multiple meanings of the basketball terms. Then he has students create for homework a graphic organizer using ten terms and their multiple meaning applications to other subject areas.

Students in every subject area benefit from the use of physical responses that complement verbal instruction. Physical Education teachers and coaches have always known the value of modeling and acting out "plays" to learn how to do them.

Students in every subject area benefit from the use of physical responses that complement verbal instruction. Physical Education teachers and coaches have always known the value of modeling and acting out "plays" to learn how to do them. Students can also use active responses to learn vocabulary and important standards in other subject areas. By creatively tying physical and active responses to learning, students master subject skills.

Students of all ages learn academic vocabulary when they become actively engaged in spelling and saying words and constructing their own meaning. Vocabulary is critical to content comprehension. The active learning of words contributes to student achievement across subject areas. Research is clear in showing the correlation between word knowledge and student achievement at every level of schooling.

Learning Skills and Content Understandings

The Best Practice teacher uses student engagement strategies first to involve students in learning interdisciplinary vocabulary words and *secondly to focus students on learning important skills and content understandings*. The teacher does this by focusing on standards-based instruction. Content lessons always begin with the vocabulary words and the targeted standard or standards. Students are asked to stand up and read the standards and then restate them in their own words. The direct instruction or *Teach* part of the lesson is introduced by having students do a quick write on what they know or have read about the content topic. Students share their responses with a partner.

Throughout the direct instruction or *Teach* part of the standards-based lesson, the teacher uses student engagement strategies to get students to think about what they are learning. Response cards can be used across subject disciplines. The 2nd grade language arts standard: *identify parts of speech including nouns and verbs* can be reinforced by having students hold up cards that say *noun* on one side and *verb* on the other in response to the teacher's list of words from a core reading selection.

After the direct instruction on the United States history standard: *Students analyze the divergent paths of the American people in the South in the mid-1800's and the challenges they faced*, the teacher can assess students learning of important concepts by having them use response cards with *valid* written on one side and *invalid* on the other.

The teacher gives facts from the history text or from readings and has students respond by holding up response cards to indicate if the factual statements or opinions are valid or invalid.

The science teacher likewise after teaching the third grade science standard: *Students know matter in three forms*, can have students hold up one of three response cards with the words, *solid, liquid and gas*. Students hold up the response cards that match the teacher's descriptions.

> **The Best Practice teacher uses student engagement strategies first to involve students in learning interdisciplinary vocabulary words and *secondly to focus students on learning important skills and content understandings*.**

Response cards can be created to reinforce content learning across subject areas. They can range from generic to specific. Two-sided generic response cards include: *agree/disagree, right/wrong. valid/invalid, true/false, correct/incorrect, fact/ opinion, fantasy/reality, question/answer, analysis/synthesis.* Two-sided language arts specific cards include: *narrative selection/expository selection, main idea/fact, compound sentence/simple sentence, metaphor/simile, past tense verb/present tense verb.* Response cards are particularly powerful in getting students to quickly generate answers. Students can then be asked to justify or evaluate their answers. The immediate feedback and discussion engages students in the learning process.

Mrs. Edna Rose is teaching her fourth grade class the English language arts standard: Distinguish between facts and opinions and cause and effect in expository text. She decides to focus on facts and opinions. The direct instruction or Teach part of the lesson consists of introducing students to the difference between facts and opinions through expository selections from: newspaper advertisements, magazines and excerpts from Internet sources. During the Practice part of the lesson she engages students by giving them Response Cards that say Fact on one side and Opinion on the other. Students are asked to confer with a partner and then hold up the correct response to statements she reads such as: All dogs are better than cats. The United States has one president. Cell phones are better than fax phones.

Students focus on the statements as they discuss them with a peer. Students have the opportunity to change their answers. Then upon a signal from the teacher, students hold up their responses. The teacher also holds up her response. Students get immediate feedback. The teacher gets a quick assessment on whether or not students have grasped the difference between a fact and an opinion. During the *Apply* part of the lesson students create their own fact and opinion statements.

Mr. Terry Adams after teaching the high school health standard: Analyze the influence of personal values and beliefs on individual health practices, engages students in the Practice part of the lesson through the use of Response Cards. Students receive cards that say correct on one side and incorrect on the other.

Mr. Adams makes a statement such as: Cultures that traditionally eat vegetables and fish have lower rates of heart disease. Students decide with a partner whether the statement is correct or incorrect. Then upon the teacher's signal, they hold up the appropriate response. Students by using response cards become actively engaged in discussions about the relationship of individual health practices and the incidences of disease (National Health Standards, 2007).

These two examples manifest how the teacher can use Response Cards across grade levels to reinforce content standards. Active discussion involves students in thinking about and applying what they are learning. They are not apathetically sitting and taking in information. They are learning by doing.

Learning by Doing

Best Practice teaching strategies *thirdly support constructivism or learning by doing.* Researchers have documented that while students retain 5% of information they learn through a lecture, they retain 95% of the information they learn when they are engaged in actively constructing knowledge. Constructivist learning involves students in making sense out of content as they experience it, evaluate it and attempt to relate it to their prior experience (Slavin, 2006).

Learning in the constructivist model is thought of as a natural ongoing social process. Learning is cyclical. It is continually reshaped, expanded and reorganized by learners. Students as they construct their own knowledge engage in wondering, questioning, forming hypothesis, communicating and investigating.

Elementary, middle school and high school students can master important science concepts through a constructivist approach to learning. Students can learn mathematics through "hands on" problem solving. They can learn important historical facts when they reenact a time in history.

Research studies confirm that principles learned through the constructivist approach are sustained over time.

Researchers have documented that while students retain 5% of information they learn through a lecture, they retain 95% of the information they learn when they are engaged in actively constructing knowledge.

Some constructivists stress the importance of social interactions during the learning by doing process, others do not. However, all agree that building knowledge actively engages students in learning across subject areas.

Levels of involvement in learning have been noted to correlate with the minimum and maximum use of cognitive processing. The use of self scoring quizzes, interactive exhibits or interactive links on the World Wide Web, correlate with increased learning. Involvement, in effect, acts as an introductory request for the cognitive processes to become activated. The "need to know" stimulates students (Carlson, 2003).

All students including English language learners profit from hands-on learning paradigms. Oral and written communication skills are advanced through active interactions with peers and multimedia sources. A three-year study by Strahan noted the benefits of learning by doing for English learners. He found that data driven dialogue and hands-on learning actually accelerated students' mastery of language patterns and vocabulary. Higher redesignation rates for English proficiency also were noted to occur (Strahan, 2004).

Fostering 21st Century Learning Paradigms

Best Practice active learning strategies fourthly foster *Best Practice 21st century learning paradigms*. These paradigms include: strategic thinking, engaging in multidisciplinary linear and nonlinear Web-based research, using electronic media for learning and using creative problem solving and applied imagination.

Mrs. Edna Drahas teaches high school world geography by using an interdisciplinary constructivist approach incorporating 21st century learning processes. She begins geography instruction by having her students create from memory an outline map of the world. She then shows students a world map and has them add missing continents to their outlines.

Mrs. Drahas focuses on the literature students are studying by having them place literature selections on the appropriate continents. She then divides students in groups. Each group selects a continent.

> *A three-year study by Strahan noted the benefits of learning by doing for English learners. He found that data driven dialogue and hands-on learning actually accelerated students' mastery of language patterns and vocabulary.*

Rather than giving students questions to answer, Mrs. Drahas has each group choose a continent to study and then compose a list of Knowledge Questions based on the five thinking themes for geography created by the National Council for Geographic Education.

The themes are:

- *Location (Where is the continent located?)*

- *Place (What makes the continent different from other continents in terms of climate and physical features?)*

- *Human Environment (What are the relationships among people living on the continent?)*

- *Movement (What are the patterns of movement of information, products or people?) Regions (How can the continent be divided in regions for study?)*

After evaluating the information related to the geographic themes for their selected continent, students use the facts they have gathered to create a strategic research question based on their interests.

One student team asks the Strategic Question: How do the geographical features of Kenya support its vision for trade in 2030? Students use information from the World Wide Web (technology) to create bar graphs and charts that manifest important facts they need to answer their Strategic Question. These facts include: population statistics, natural resources allocations, products exported and imported and yearly weather conditions. (math) Students create surveys that they can use to interview selected Kenyans over email to get first hand information on the country's implementation of trade policies. (social science) They also use blogging to communicate with groups of students in the country to explore pertinent environmental issues. (science).

Finally, students integrate their research to answer their Strategic Question. The answer may include a solution to challenges that can be shared across continents with their student peers.

Students may also use their research to create new scenarios for intercontinental trade in 2030 using their applied imaginations.

By structuring their own learning activities, students engage in 21st century interdisciplinary learning. They gather information from both linear and nonlinear formats including the World Wide Web. They apply both analytic and creative thinking to answer the strategic question they themselves have posed.

By becoming actively engaged in learning, students acquire more information than they would from passively reading a geography text.

Another high school teacher, Mr. Lee McBride, engages his students by having them experience geography through the eyes of migrating whales. By studying the migratory routes of five different whales, students learn about the continents of the world and the countries within them. Students understand the placement of the oceans by exploring the trips whales make as they migrate from one end of the world to another. The study of geography is extended to multidisciplinary learning including math and science. Students study the whales' body structure, eating habits and reproduction (McBride, 2003).

Student Engagement and Interactive Electronic Media

Best Practice student engagement strategies combine 21st century learning paradigms with electronic media applications. Mr. McBride's geography lesson using migratory whales can be extended by having students use specific Web sites and links to find information on whales. Students can be asked to create bar graphs or spread sheets to report the information they have found.

Mr. McBride's lesson can be supported by computer games and other informational links on the World Wide Web. There are many links that students can use to pursue further knowledge not only on geography but on the interdisciplinary aspects of the lesson as well. Games and activities on the internet range in difficulty. While English learners benefit from games that teach vocabulary through categorization of mammals, more sophisticated learners profit from interactive sites where they learn and apply scientific principles. Web-based games also have the advantage of using principles of cognitive science to engage students in learning. These games require students to think complexly and creatively.

Web-based games also have the advantage of using principles of cognitive science to engage students in learning. These games require students to think complexly and creatively.

Encouraging Creative Problem Solving and Applied Imagination

Creative problem solving and applied imagination are hallmarks of 21st century learning. Interdisciplinary questions that promote creative, imaginative thinking include: What if_____? What can you invent to change_____? How can you synthesize these facts to create something new? What is an equally valued alternative perspective?

Divergent thinking and applied imagination stretch ideas from the mundane to the possible. Knowledge becomes more usable when it is imaginatively synthesized and dynamically extended.

Miss Eileen Lynch encourages her students to use applied imagination in open-ended learning activities. The goal of all the exercises is to have students quickly generate as many ideas as possible without restrictions. Today students have studied the vocabulary word "ridiculous." Miss Lynch gives her class the following task: List all the words, phrases, and figures of speech including idioms that you can think of which might be used instead of the word, ridiculous. This exercise has no right or wrong answers. It encourages students to stretch the limits of their vocabulary knowledge. Another exercise she uses in math involves students in creating at least three different ways to portray the same answer.

Just as there are exercises to develop a great, agile body, applied imagination exercises help students develop a great, agile mind.

Although the skill of using applied imagination looks easy on the surface, it is a creative problem solving skill that must be developed. Just as there are exercises to develop a great, agile body, applied imagination exercises help students develop a great, agile mind.

The Best Practice teacher creates the optimum learning environment for students through the application of student engagement strategies that: *involve students in the learning process; focus students on learning important skills and content understandings; support constructivism or learning by doing;*

foster 21st century learning paradigms; and support learning with electronic media. An active learning environment can be implemented in the classroom by dividing the day into:

1. *direct instruction time* where students are engaged by: making active and observable physical responses, signaling by hand responses, holding up response cards, answering chorally, penning quick writes, taking written notes and creating graphic organizers;

2. *practice opportunities* where students work with partners to master content standards;

3. *academic learning by doing* where students are engaged in authentic interdisciplinary learning experiences that incorporate electronic media;

4. creative problem solving and applied imagination exercises where students have the opportunity to stretch their thinking to create new paradigms.

Ultimately, the more time students spend engaged in active knowledge building activities, the more they learn. Increased learning results in higher student achievement across subject disciplines and on high stakes testing.

Think About Discussion Questions

1. Find two games on the World Wide Web that would support students' learning one of the content standards that you teach.

2. Create an applied imagination exercise that you can use with the content area you teach or with one of the content areas you teach to stretch students' imaginations. (See page 91)

Reflection on Student Engagement and Achievement

1. Reflect on what you read in this chapter about 21st century learning. What argument could you make to support the following claim: *Imagination is more important than knowledge?* (Einstein)

2. Evaluate the time you spend on constructivist activities and creative problem solving in your classroom. Then analyze your daily lesson plans. Reflect on how you can integrate more constructivist activities into your daily or weekly schedule.

Chapter 5

Best Practices Cooperative Discussion Strategies

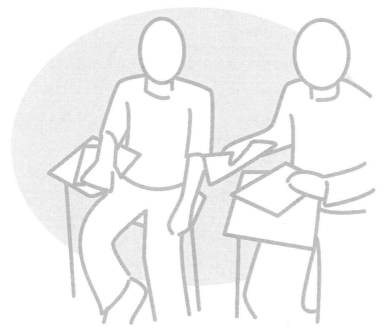

As Mrs. Glenda Gritton teaches a lesson on United States history, she poses higher level thinking questions to her class. Instead of asking individual students to answer each question, she uses the Best Practice Think-Pair-Share technique.

She asks: "What would have been the likely outcome if the United States had maintained its isolationist position and not entered World War II?"

She says: "Tell your partner what you think the outcome of World War II might have been."

Cooperative Discussion Strategies for Student Engagement

- What are cooperative discussion strategies?

- How does Think-Pair-Share engage students in cooperative discussions?

- How does jigsaw engage groups in content discussions?

- Why does brainstorming encourage cooperative thinking and the generation of ideas?

- How does whiteboarding engage students in content learning?

- How do graphic organizers including T charts, Y charts and PMI tables encourage students to think and share?

Research shows that the active thinking and sharing process actually increases students' engagement in learning and content comprehension. Furthermore, students who are exposed to the Think-Pair-Share strategy on a consistent basis increase their retention of information by up to 95%.

Cooperative discussion strategies intensely engage students in sharing and applying what they are learning. Students interact with peers in focused discussions. They apply what they are learning to answer questions and solve problems. Best Practice cooperative discussion strategies that foster active learning include: *Think-Pair-Share, Jigsaw, Brainstorming, Using Whiteboards and Sharing Thoughts with Graphic Organizers.*

The *Think-Pair-Share* cooperative discussion strategy actively engages students in learning subject matter content. The Best Practice teacher, during direct content-based instruction, uses the *Think-Pair-Share* strategy by posing a challenging open-ended question. Students are given time to think about the question and share their responses with their partners. This sharing process forces students to think about what they are learning.

Research shows that the active thinking and sharing process actually increases students' engagement in learning and content comprehension. Furthermore, students who are exposed to the *Think-Pair-Share* strategy on a consistent basis increase their retention of information by up to 95% (Vaca, 2002).

Mr. Brian Castro is beginning a lesson on the English language arts standard: Use a dictionary to learn the meaning and other features of unknown words. He begins the lesson by posing this open-ended question to the class: Why do you think dictionaries are important? He gives students time to think about their answers. Students are then given time to talk to a partner. After the paired interaction, students share their responses with the class.

Mr. Castro implements the four steps of the *Think-Pair-Share* strategy in his lesson on the significance of dictionaries. It is important to note that each step has a time limit which is signaled by the teacher. The timed steps in the *Think-Pair-Share* strategy are organized around the thinking process. The thinking process includes time to reflect and time to share. Students are given usually about one to two minutes to reflect on their answers. Then students are given another one to two minutes to share their thinking and get immediate feedback from a peer.

The *Best Practice* Teacher gets optimum results from the *Think-Pair-Share* strategy by following the four implementation steps.

Ask an Open Ended Question

Step One—The teacher asks an open-ended question where there is not just one right answer.

The first step in the *Think-Pair-Share* process is for the teacher to ask an open-ended question. This step is important because it sets the purpose for learning. The question serves as an anticipatory set to engage students. As students answer Mr. Castro's question, *Why are dictionaries important?*, they determine the purpose for learning the ELA standard that targets using the dictionary.

The teacher can also ask questions that extend students' thinking. For example, *How can you learn new vocabulary by using the dictionary? What clues does the dictionary give you for decoding and understanding new words?*

The Think Part of Think-Pair-Share

Step Two—Students think individually. This is the Think part of the Think-Pair Share.

A signal is used to indicate that students have time to reflect upon the posed question. Students are given the limit of one to two minutes of think time. Providing the wait time of one to two minutes increases the quality of students' responses. Research confirms that when students are given time to mentally "chew on questions" they respond more clearly. Wait time also helps students to become more actively involved in the lesson (Lyman, 1987).

Think-Write-Pair-Share

Providing the wait time of one to two minutes increases the quality of students' responses. Research confirms when students are given time to mentally "chew on questions" they respond more clearly.

It may be helpful, though not necessary, for students in step two to be given the opportunity to write out their answers. Visual learners seem to prefer this type of "written thinking." Whether the answer is thought about or written about, students must understand that there is no one right answer. It is essential, however, that everyone come up with an answer to the teacher's question.

The Pair-Share Part of Think-Pair-Share

Step Three—Students discuss their answers with a partner. This is the Pair-Share part of the Think-Pair Share.

Using designated partners or near by neighbors, students begin to talk over their answers. They compare their mental and written notes and identify the answers they think are best, most convincing, or most unique. During the *Pair-Share* students can try out possibilities. Students together can reformulate a common answer based on their collective insights.

As students talk over ideas, they are forced to use their prior knowledge. Their misunderstandings about the topic are revealed during this discussion stage. Students also are more likely to participate in the discussion with one person rather than initially having to share their answers with the whole class.

Pair-Shares are a good time to match English learners with proficient English speakers. Students learn the second language most expediently through conversations and focused dialogue.

At times it may be beneficial to group English language learners into foursomes. This often encourages more shared dialogue and conversation. It also allows *Crystallizers* more time to sit and listen to group responses, if they are not ready yet to share.

The Class Share Part of Think-Pair-Share

Step Four—Students share their answers with the whole class. This is the Share part of the Think-Pair-Share strategy.

After students share in pairs, the teacher calls on pairs to share their thinking with the rest of the class. Pairs may choose to present their responses verbally or in the form of a visual or graphic. Preferred learning modalities can be used by students to explain the ideas behind their answers. Most importantly, the ideas are embedded in the language of the learners rather than the language of the teacher or the textbook.

Think-Pair-Share engages all students in active cooperative discussion. Meaningful dialogue creates what the word dialogue means "a flow of meaning." By actively creating their own meaning, students retain more and achieve more. Students become active thinkers rather than passive receptors.

Research studies have shown that the teacher's use of the *Think-Pair-Share strategy* increases on task behavior and decreases off task behavior. Accountability is built into the model because each student must report to a partner, and partners must report to the class. Each part of the process of *Think-Pair-Share* builds in *Best Practices* for learning. The *Think* step builds in wait time which is a researched-based Best Practice. It gives students time to access their background knowledge. It also gives English language learners time to process the information.

The *Pair-Share* step builds in the Best Practice of cooperative group discussion. Students all share their thinking about the teacher's question. The *Share* part of the lesson gives students the opportunity to try out their answers on a partner before going "public" and sharing them with the rest of the class.

> *Think-Pair-Share engages all students in active cooperative discussion. Meaningful dialogue creates what the word dialogue means "a flow of meaning." By actively creating their own meaning, students retain more and achieve more. Students become active thinkers rather than passive receptors.*

Sharing answers with a partner often causes students to rethink and rework their responses. Sharing motivates students to apply the 21st century skill of applied imagination by creating new ways of looking at old problems or information. The old adage applies here: "two heads are better than one."

Finally, the *Think-Pair-Share* strategy builds on the Best Practice of learning by doing. It breaks up lengthy lectures by having students become active participants in learning. Students' active thinking is initiated by the teacher's question. This means that students' thinking can only be as good as the question the teacher poses in Step One. Lower level questions do not prompt the level of thought that higher level questions demand. It is the higher level questions that promote students' best thinking and creating.

> *Lower level questions do not prompt the level of thought that higher level questions demand. It is the higher level questions that promote students' best thinking and creating.*

The thinking process promoted by the *Think-Pair-Share* strategy can be implemented across subject areas. Students can solve math problems on their own and then swap solutions with a partner. Students can check each others' answers before the problems are reviewed by the class. Students can discuss how to rename fractions or talk over the steps of an algebra problem. *Think-Pair-Share* can be used for students to plan out science experiments. Students can create graphs and charts together. They can analyze diets or review the body systems. They can also share responses to literature or expository text selections. *Think-Pair-Share* is a powerful student engagement strategy that can be applied to all content standards-based learning.

Applying Think-Pair-Share to Content Standards-based Learning

The *Think-Pair-Share* strategy can be used very effectively with the English language arts standards that address writing. Students can write independently and then share their work with a partner. They can serve as each others' editors. The final edited product can be shared with the class. Another writing application of *Think-Pair-Share* is to provide pairs of students with a transparency and overhead pen. This allows students to prepare a written visual to share with the class.

The strategy can be applied to spelling, as well as writing. Students can be given time to think about the spelling of words. After reflecting upon the word's configuration, they spell the word to a partner. The partner gives a "thumbs up" to show agreement with the spelling or corrects the spelling.

Think-Pair-Share can be used for summarizing narratives or solving a math problem. Students first read a passage or solve a problem. They then think about a summary of the passage or a solution to the problem. Finally, they share their summary or their solution with a partner. *Think-Pair-Share* also lends itself well to science or history expository reading. Students can think about and then create with a partner a graphic organizer to categorize the expository text information.

Students' participation in *Think-Pair-Share* strategy engages them in applying the 21st century skills of synthesis and applied imagination. After students have thought about how to integrate ideas into a persuasive essay or a mini ad campaign, they consult with a partner. They then create a finished product using their combined thinking.

There are a number of management techniques that optimize the use of the Think-Pair-Share strategy include: assigning partners before beginning the activity, switching discussion partners, monitoring discussions by walking around the room and calling randomly on student pairs during class sharing.

The successful implementation of the *Think-Pair-Share* strategy in the classroom requires good management skills. There are a number of management techniques that optimize the use of the *Think-Pair-Share* strategy. These techniques include: assigning partners in the beginning, rather than saying talk to a partner, switching discussion partners so that students can hear different perspectives, monitoring discussions by walking around the room and finally calling randomly on student pairs during class sharing. These management strategies enable the teacher to keep students engaged and on task.

Jigsaw a Cooperative Discussion Student Engagement Strategy

Jigsaw, like *Think-Pair-Share*, is a cooperative discussion Best Practice strategy for engaging students in learning. The jigsaw strategy was developed in 1978 by Aronson as a group discussion technique. This strategy is analogous to a jigsaw puzzle. Students research pieces of a subject topic in groups. Then the pieces are put together in the form of peer teaching. Just as in a jigsaw puzzle, each piece, each student's part, is essential for the completion and full understanding of the final product.

> **The jigsaw strategy is analogous to a jigsaw puzzle. Students research pieces of a subject topic in groups. Then the pieces are put together in the form of peer teaching.**

Mr. Marcos Avila is teaching United States history. He uses the jigsaw technique to involve his students in a discussion of World War II. First, he puts students in teams of four. Then he assigns each member of the group a topic relating to World War II. Mr. Avila expects students to become experts on their assigned topics. Team one members have different assignments.

Maria's topic is Adolph Hitler's rise to power in prewar Germany. Marcos has a topic relating to Britain's role in World War II. Sao will research the Soviet Union's participation in WWII. Millie has the assignment of finding out about Japan's entry into the war. The other teams have members with the same topics.

Members of the teams (one from each team) with the same topic meet together in an expert group. For example, students assigned to Britain's role in World War II meet as a team of specialists. They gather information from a variety of resource materials including the internet and texts. The expert group works to put together the information they have researched.

Finally, the students from each expert group return to their jigsaw teams to report what they have learned. The expert on Japan teaches the other group members what he or she has learned. The other topic experts in each group educate the whole team on their specialty. Team members take notes. After each expert in the jigsaw group shares information on one topic, the information is put together like pieces of a puzzle in an integrated report.

The *Jigsaw* methodology employed by Mr. Avila is a research-based Best Practice strategy with a track record of promoting student engagement and academic achievement. This cooperative learning strategy is effective because it engages each student as an important contributor of needed information. It also promotes 21ˢᵗ century team learning. Members of expert teams must work together to research information about a topic. *Jigsaw* groups are dependent on the expert members to give them all the pieces of information to complete the puzzle. Communication and cooperation are essential for team members to integrate the research into a final report.

> *Jigsaw groups are dependent on the expert members to give them all the pieces of information to complete the puzzle. Communication and cooperation are essential for team members to integrate the research into a final report.*

The *Jigsaw* strategy promotes the 21ˢᵗ century skill of interdisciplinary learning. For example, the topic of rain forests can be explored from interdisciplinary perspectives. One expert group can study rainforests from a geographical perspective. They can draw maps depicting the locations of rainforests on the world's continents. Another expert group can study rainforests from a mathematical perspective. They can apply their math skills to create graphs and charts on the destruction of rain forests. A third expert group can approach the study of rain forests from an environmentalist perspective. This group can write a persuasive essay on the reasons to preserve rainforests. The fourth expert group can behave like historians finding out information about rainforests from a historical perspective. The fifth expert group can adopt a scientific perspective. They can take on the roles of scientists to study how plants in the rain forests are used for medicine.

Engaging students in cooperative interdisciplinary learning using the *Jigsaw strategy* increases student achievement.

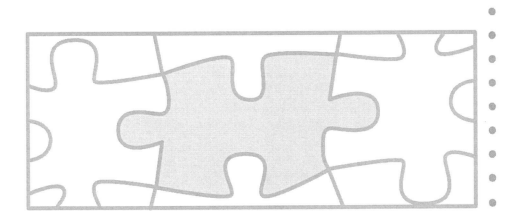

Setting up a Class Jigsaw

The teacher can maximize learning by following the five steps to setting up a class jigsaw:

1. Divide the class into four or five teams. Assign each group member a topic.

2. Members of teams with the same topic meet together in expert groups. A variety of research materials, as well as the internet, are made available to expert groups. Expert groups are directed to use these resources to find information about their topic.

3. Experts return to jigsaw teams to teach what they have learned to peers.

4. Team members listen and take notes on the information taught by peers.

5. Students write a group report integrating the pieces of information they have learned from the experts. Students can also be given a test on the topic (Rudell, 2003).

> **Students write a group report integrating the pieces of information they have learned from the experts. Students can also be given a test on the topic.**

Jigsaw grouping as a cooperative learning strategy has technology applications. Roseman designed *PoetryQuest.net* using *Jigsaw* grouping to teach the concepts of poetry (Roseman, 2006). She arranged students in teams of five. Then she had group members go to the WebQuest to get information on one topic of poetry. After studying poetry using the WebQuest, students taught fellow team members what they learned. A list of jigsaw Web Quests can be found in the appendix of this book.

Brainstorming and Student Engagement

Brainstorming encourages the same cooperative thinking seen in jigsaws. The technique of brainstorming promotes the thinking process without restrictions. This means there are no right or wrong answers. Brainstorming, in fact, encourages "wild ideas." Judgment of ideas is withheld. Students are encouraged to piggyback on the ideas of others.

> *Mrs. Ada Guido is beginning the process of creative writing with her second-grade class. She poses the open-ended question: What if everything in the world was green? Students are given time to think about the question and to brainstorm with a partner. Maria and her partner come to the conclusion that it would be a world without rainbows. Arthur and his partner say the world would look like a bowl of peas. Mrs. Guido accepts all ideas without judgment or criticism. She writes the ideas of all student pairs on the whiteboard. She encourages all students to participate in generating ideas about a green world. Even James, a shy student, piggybacks on the bowl of peas' idea by saying the world's oceans then would look like pea soup.*

The purpose of *Brainstorming* is to focus cooperative discussions on the process of idea generation. While creative students use idea generation naturally, all students can be taught this technique. The advantage of learning to generate ideas has implications for all subject areas. Idea generation is important before beginning the writing process. It is also necessary for problem solving and coming up with creative solutions.

Brainstorming along with applied imagination is part of the creative process. It is a 21st century skill. It encourages students to use all the facts at their disposal to come up with new ways of doing things. Brainstorming helps students find solutions to learning challenges. It engages students in learning and accelerates student achievement. Students who can brainstorm and generate ideas score higher on high stakes tests and on writing prompts (Dale, 2005).

> **The technique of brainstorming promotes the thinking process without restrictions. This means there are no right or wrong answers. Brainstorming, in fact, encourages "wild ideas." Judgement of ideas is withheld.**

Student Engagement and Whiteboards

Brainstorming can be done on *Whiteboards*. Some students feel more comfortable with written idea generation. Using whiteboards for brainstorming is another Best Practice student engagement strategy. Whiteboards are the 21st century version of the chalk slates used by students in colonial times. They provide a great way of actively engaging students in the learning process. Whiteboards are also a terrific tool for immediate feedback and assessment (MacIsaac, 2006).

Mrs. Elizabeth Charles has her high school algebra students use large 24"x 32" whiteboards that are cut from white economy tile board for brainstorming during group problem solving. Mrs. Charles likes the large whiteboards because she can more easily see a group's thinking.

Today, she is targeting the algebra 1 mathematical reasoning standard: Students solve multistep word problems involving linear equations and linear inequalities. As Mrs. Charles walks around the room, she notices the different ways students are making use of the whiteboards. James as the Team leader of Group 2 has divided the large whiteboard into sections to lay out the steps for solving the word problems.

Mr. Jaime Castro uses whiteboards with his third-grade students as a student engagement strategy. He has students solve standards-based story problems in response to a prompt. At his signal, students hold up their whiteboards. Students explain their thinking to a partner. Mr. Castro then shows the right answer. Students have the opportunity to correct wrong answers. Whiteboards give Mr. Castro immediate feedback on what his students know. This enables him to target instruction for students needing extra help.

While Mrs. Charles uses large whiteboards as a cooperative group student engagement strategy with her high school algebra students, Mr. Castro uses individual whiteboards to engage his elementary students in problem solving.

The benefit of both types of whiteboards is the ease of modification. Students often are more willing to take risks if they know they can modify their answers. Ideas can be exposed, discussed, accepted and discarded with the flexibility of a whiteboard.

Whiteboards are the 21st century version of the chalk slates used by students in colonial times. They provide a great way of actively engaging students in the learning process. Whiteboards are also a terrific tool for immediate feedback and assessment.

Whiteboards facilitate student interaction and support a 21st century constructivist approach to learning. Students use whiteboards as tools for creation and as a prop for discussion and idea sharing. The Best Practice teacher further facilitates group sharing of large whiteboards through a *museum walk* (students silently walk from board to board) and hear group presentations (Henry, 2006).

There are endless uses of whiteboards for individual, paired and group learning. White boards can be used for the *Practice* part of any lesson. Students can dictate and write spelling words on whiteboards or engage in cooperative problem solving.

Whiteboards are excellent tools for English language learners. Whiteboards are particularly powerful with *Crystallizers* who may feel uncomfortable taking verbal risks. They, however, often feel more comfortable with answers that can be modified and erased. Whiteboards can be used with English learners for verb practice. The teacher can have students conjugate verbs and then create a sentence with a partner. Whiteboards facilitate the teaching of grammatical order. English language learners can be asked to change statements into questions. The teacher can reinforce word order by writing words on whiteboards for students to arrange into a sentence. Whiteboards lend themselves well to the *Rule of 3* for vocabulary development. After spelling and saying the word, students can write the word on the whiteboard, tell the definition to a partner and then create an image on the whiteboard that depicts the meaning of the word.

Finally, whiteboards can be effectively used for student note taking and for question generating during the direct instruction part of the lesson. Students can easily write down key concepts or facts. Whiteboards also facilitate the question generating process as students can immediately note what puzzles them or what they need more information about.

Sharing Thoughts with Graphic Organizers

Graphic organizers encourage learners to work together to visually record their thinking on a topic. Visual images help students establish connections and make relationships between different concepts and ideas. Graphic organizers can be created by a group on a large whiteboard, on paper, or on the computer.

> *Graphic organizers encourage learners to work together to visually record their thinking on a topic. Visual images help students establish connections and make relationships between different concepts and ideas. Graphic organizers can be created by a group on a large whiteboard, on paper, or on the computer.*

A *T chart* is one of the many graphic organizers. It can be used for groups to list the pros and cons about a controversial topic in science or in any other subject area. The controversial issue of using stem cells from human embryos lends itself well to a group discussion using a *T chart*. The following is an example:

Cell Stem Research

Pros	Cons
1. stem cell research gives us information on the basics of the body	1. ethical issues outweigh the benefits
2. stem cells can be used to treat medical problems	2. scientific value has been overstated
3. stem cells have the potential to cure diseases like Alzheimer	3. an embryo is a potential life

A *Y chart* is an extension of a *T chart*. Students can use a *Y chart* for group discussions that extend their thinking. The following is an example of a Y chart that can be implemented after the reading of a poem to describe the wind.

The Wind in the Poem
feels like

looks like   *sounds like*

PMI or (*Plus, Minus, Intriguing*) is a graphic organizer that can be used for information processing. Students can discuss the pluses, minuses and intriguing aspects in a lesson, concept or issue (Bellanca, 1998). This is an example of the *PMI* graphic organizer on the science topic of endangered species.

What we liked *(Pluses)*	*Ways to protect endangered animals.*
What we didn't like *(Minuses)*	*The number of animals becoming extinct.*
What we thought was intriguing *(Questions or Thoughts)*	*Why are some rainforest animals becoming endangered species?*

The Best Practice teacher encourages students to utilize *T Charts*, *Y charts* and *PMI* graphic organizers to document and clarify their thinking. *Brainstorming*, *Whiteboards*, *Jigsawing* and *Think-Pair-Share* strategies are also implemented in the classroom to engage students in the learning process through group discussion.

Think About Discussion Questions

1. Create a standards-based activity using the PMI graphic organizer on page 108 to reinforce a content standard you teach. Use the activity with your class and write a short reflection.

2. Think about how you would implement the *Think-Write-Pair-Share* strategy in the subject area you teach. Implement the strategy with your class. Then use a *T chart* to list the pros and cons of using the strategy with your students.

Reflection on Engaging Students Using Best Practice Cooperative Discussion Strategies

1. Reflect on the student engagement strategies in this chapter. Choose two of the student engagement strategies discussed. Write a persuasive paragraph to convince your colleagues to use these strategies.

2. Reflect on how you think the jigsaw strategy prepares students for the teamwork required in the 21st century workforce.

Chapter 6

Power Learning and Student Engagement Strategies

Three Person Read is a student engagement strategy that helps students master subject content. This strategy begins by the teacher grouping students in teams of three. Each person on a team reads one part of a longer subject area selection. Students make main ideas and details outlines. Then each person on the team teaches the main ideas and the most significant details to the two other members. Each person quizzes the other members to make sure they know all the parts.

Power Learning and Student Engagement

- *What student engagement strategies can the teacher use to create Power Learners?*

- *How does the teacher foster self-directed learning and accelerated achievement through the use of student engagement strategies?*

- *What strategies support students learning specific skills and content-based standards?*

- *What do students need to learn to become self-directed learners?*

> **Power Learning and student engagement are intricately connected. Students become engaged when they direct their own learning.**

Power Learning and student engagement are intricately connected. Students become engaged when they direct their own learning. The majority of students do not enter the classroom as *Power Learners*. They become Power Learners through the process of active, accelerated learning.

Learners become focused and energized when they are engaged in active group investigations. They become intrinsically motivated by curiosity, interest and discovery.

They use their creative thinking skills to make choices on how to apply knowledge. They have productive, meaningful discussions with peers that lead to problem solving. Students who become engaged in these activities achieve at higher levels in school.

As students participate in active group investigations, they learn to take on roles as members of a team. Students learn the importance of idea sharing and consensus building which is a 21st century skill.

The Best Practice teacher facilitates the process of active team learning through the classroom implementation of student engagement strategies that: *activate prior knowledge, foster active investigation, promote the active mastery of the content standards, allow for choice, include games and humor, promote group interaction, encourage collaboration, nature higher level thinking and monitor student accountability* (Jablon, 2006). It is the implementation of these strategies that leads to accelerated or *Power Learning*.

Activating Prior Knowledge and Power Learning

Strategies that *activate prior knowledge* are some of the most important for engaging students in Power Learning. Students become more engaged when learning is scaffolded on what they know. This is particularly important in classrooms with diverse learners who bring different background experiences to learning. By understanding students' readiness levels, teachers can scaffold instruction to the next level. This holds true for all content instruction.

In order to target instruction, the teacher needs to know what understandings and skills learners bring to subject-matter topics. A classic student engagement strategy that gives the teacher information on the student's knowledge base is KWL.

KWL Student Engagement Strategy

Before beginning a new topic of study in English language arts, Mr. Tony Romero asks students to write what they Know about the topic, what they Wonder about the topic and what they want to Learn. Today the topic for his eighth-graders is a literature selection on Martin Luther King, Jr. Mr. Romero is surprised to learn that some of his students' grandparents actually took part in marches and demonstrations. These students tell other students what they Know about the harrowing experiences of their family members as they campaigned to end segregation.

Students become more engaged in reading a selection when they are reading to answer questions in which they are interested. They are less engaged when they are directed to answer less relevant questions posed by the textbook or the teacher.

Students in Mr. Romero's class Wonder why there was segregation in the first place. Others wonder if segregation still exists in parts of the United States. They wonder if the end of segregation must go beyond being mandated. They wonder if segregation happens every time someone does not want to interact with someone who is different from them in some way. In many ways, they wonder if segregation does not even exist on their school campus.

As students discuss what they Wonder about, they decide they want to Learn more about the Civil Rights movement and Martin Luther King, Jr.'s life. They want to know why Martin Luther King, Jr. was so committed to ending segregation that he risked his life and the lives of his family. Another aspect they are curious about is why Martin Luther King, Jr. choose the approach of peaceful nonresistance.

By finding out what students *Know, Wonder about* and want to *Learn*, Mr. Romero can build on their prior knowledge and emphasize the topic selections that answer students' questions and concerns. Students become more engaged in reading a selection when they are reading to answer questions in which they are interested. They are less engaged when they are directed to answer less relevant questions posed by the textbook or the teacher. No matter how good a textbook is, the textbook cannot get into students' heads. Especially considering that the information in students' heads may be tied to cultural and individual family experiences that are different than those of the textbook author or the teacher. It is this information in students' heads that is the foundation for Power Learning. Students expand their background knowledge across subject areas through active investigations.

Active Investigation: Creating Alternative Strategies and Solutions

Student engagement activities that foster *finding alternative strategies and solutions to problems* also encourage *Power Learning.* Many students fail to become Power Learners because they are rarely presented with opportunities to explore a topic from multiple perspectives. It is less frequently that they are asked open-ended questions. Too much emphasis on the one right answer has a negative impact on students. Oftentimes, the one right answer set transfers into situations where it is inappropriate because there can be several right answers (Hunter and Hunter, 2004).

Students who are scripted to find one right answer fail to seek out alterative solutions. They are unmotivated to engage in higher level possibility thinking. It is this possibility thinking that leads to success in the 21st century workforce where seeking new and alternative solutions is the norm rather than the exception.

Mr. Arnold Korn uses the student engagement strategy entitled Multiple Solutions to foster students' creation of alterative strategies and solutions. He begins lessons by asking students these types of questions: How many ways can you create shapes on these geoboards? Do you think there are more coins in the jar or in the glass? How can you organize this data on car accidents per mile to predict future accidents? Does the answer to this problem prove the math principle we learned? ? Why or Why not? Who has an idea how to solve this algebra equation? Who has a different idea?

Many students fail to become Power Learners because they are rarely presented with opportunities to explore a topic from multiple perspectives.

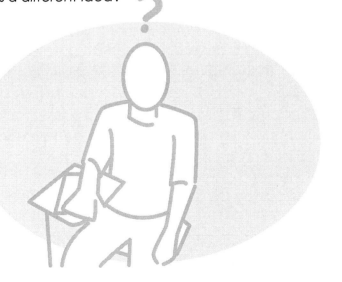

Student Engagement Strategies for Active Investigation

The *Multiple Solutions* strategy engages students as they answer the open-ended questions posed by Mr. Korn. This active investigation student engagement strategy may be used at the beginning, in the practice part, or at the end of a lesson.

RoundAbout, Four Corners and *Send a Question* are additional student engagement strategies that encourage multiple answers, strategic questioning and alternative solutions. The *RoundAbout* strategy begins by the teacher putting students in teams. The teacher then asks a question that has many possible answers. Using a sheet of paper, students make a list of answers. Each person adds one answer and then passes the paper to the person to his or her left. The *RoundAbout* strategy focuses students on alternative answers to questions as they read their peers' responses.

The *Four Corners* strategy is especially effective in situations where students are reading about controversial or thought-provoking topics. A debatable statement is given by the teacher for students to think about, such as: *All students should be required to take three years of science in high school.*

After thinking about the teacher's statement, students are directed to stand in one of the four corners of the classroom which are labeled: *Strongly Agree, Agree, Strongly Disagree, Disagree.* Students in each corner state their reasoning and gather facts to defend their position. Each group presents their reasoning along with their facts to the other groups. The goal is for a group to present a powerful enough argument to motivate other students to reconsider their thinking. Students may indeed change groups at any time. This engagement strategy can be used from elementary school to high school. It is an important strategy because it encourages students to analyze and evaluate their thinking.

The Four Corners strategy is especially effective in situations where students are reading about controversial or thought-provoking topics. A debatable statement is given by the teacher for students to think about, such as: All students should be required to take three years of science in high school.

The *Send a Question* student engagement strategy can be used to reinforce student mastery of a content standard, such as the 8th grade history standard: *Students analyze the divergent paths of the American people in the West from 1800 to the mid-1800s and the challenges they faced.*

After direct instruction on the history content standard, students are placed in teams. Each team writes a series of five open-ended questions on flashcards that relate to what they learned about the challenges of living in the West in the 1800's. Questions on this topic might include: What challenges led to women gaining new status in the West? How did the concept of Manifest Destiny effect the settlement of the West? Each team's questions are passed on from team to team. Team members share their thinking to arrive at consensus to answer the questions. Students become engaged through the Send a Question strategy as they create their own questions and answer their peer's questions. They use the 21st century skills of synthesizing information and consensus-building.

Detective is a student engagement strategy that the teacher can use at the beginning of a lesson. The primary purpose of this strategy is to have students begin study on a new topic by doing research. For example, a history lesson on the causes of the Civil War would not commence with having students read the chapter. It would begin by having students become detectives *to see what they can find out* about the Civil War.

Active Investigation: Generalizing Results of Problem Solving Activities

Science investigations and interdisciplinary problem solving activities engage students in the process of problem solving and making generalizations. Students discover principles that they can use across disciplines.

Students in Miss Jenny Waters's kindergarten class are learning the Life Science Content Standard: *Students know how to observe and describe similarities and differences in the appearance and behavior of plants and animals.* They have learned some generalizations about fish. Groups of students are discussing whether to classify animals as fish based on the generalizations they have learned including: It lives in water; It has fins; It breathes with gills and it gets oxygen from the water.

Applying generalizations in different situations helps students become Power Learners. When students learn to focus on key understandings, they develop the ability to ignore distractions. They also learn to apply the higher level thinking skills of analyzing and evaluating.

High school students in Mr. Robert Jefferson's class are learning the Earth Science Content Standard: Astronomy and planetary exploration reveal the solar system's structure, scale and change over time. Mr. Jefferson has integrated English language arts standards into the science lesson. These include: Develop presentations by using clear research questions and creative and critical research strategies. Integrate databases, graphics and spreadsheets into word-processed documents.

Mr. Jefferson tells students they are going to study information on the solar system and use research from geological studies that suggest that early Earth was very different from the Earth today. The changes of Earth over time is to be documented by students on charts. Students as a group are to formulate a Strategic Research Question that relates to this topic and a number of Knowledge Questions that are needed to clarify the answer to their Strategic Question.

> *Applying generalizations in different situations helps students become Power Learners. When students learn to focus on key understandings, they develop the ability to ignore distractions.*

Mr. Jefferson has assigned a Team Leader to each group. Students are to research the answer to their Strategic Question by assuming one of the following roles: statistician, geologist, biologist, ecologist and anthropologist. Research must be conducted using both text information and information from the World Wide Web.

Students are given the scientific vocabulary words to complement their research. They are to use these words to help them gain a conceptual understanding of the process of the Earth's evolution. Students are also instructed by Mr. Jefferson to use both qualitative observation skills and quantitative skills in researching databases and Web sites. Research is to be documented by students through the use of spreadsheets, graphic organizers and sequenced written reports.

Team Leaders are to evaluate their group's progress on an assessment rubric. Mr. Jefferson serves as a learning facilitator. He establishes a time frame for the learning assignment. He meets with groups to help them formulate their Strategic Research Question. He facilitates the inquiry process by suggesting ideas and direction for accessing information. He enables students to construct their own understandings on the Earth through methods of scientific inquiry.

Research on Cooperative Grouping affirms that arranging students in teams has a powerful effect on students' engagement in learning (Lou, 2006).

Cooperative Grouping and Power Learning

Mr. Jefferson in this example successfully implements the research-based engagement strategy entitled Cooperative Grouping. There are five essential factors that optimize this type of learning arrangement: 1) The targeted standard is posted for students; 2) Both text and nonlinear assignments are used; 3) A Team Leader is assigned to each group; 4) A time frame is established for assignment completion; 5) An assessment rubric is used both for group and teacher evaluation.

Research on Cooperative Grouping affirms that arranging students in teams has a powerful effect on students' engagement in learning (Lou, 2006).

Studies further verify that students who participate in team learning achieve at higher levels than those who work alone (Marzano, 2001). This is especially true when students are graded as a team rather than individually. Small teams of three to four members are reported to keep students more engaged than larger groups.

Formal Cooperative Strategies and Student Engagement

The *Best Practice* teacher can engage students through the use of formal cooperative learning groups and informal collaborative pairings. One formal cooperative grouping strategy is called *Numbered Heads Together*. This strategy is especially helpful for reviewing concepts after a unit of study. The implementation of this strategy includes these three steps:

1) Number off students in each group, up to four. The teacher or the students can assign the numbers.

2) Ask students a question or give them a problem to solve. Students put their heads together to answer the question.

3) Call on a number to act as spokesperson for the group.

The Numbered Heads Together strategy ensures that each group member knows the answers to questions related to a unit of study. Students as they interact with their peers take responsibility for their own learning (Terezini, 2005).

Ms. Claudia Lopez, an algebra teacher, uses a variation of the Numbered Heads strategy which she terms Challenge Numbered Heads. She uses the strategy to get students to practice the Algebra I Math Content Standard: Students solve equations and inequalities involving absolute values. After teaching the standard, Mrs. Lopez numbers off students in groups of six. She gives groups equations to solve. After giving these teams of students time to solve the equations, she rolls two different colored dice to indicate which team and which team member will be called upon to respond to her question. Groups are told as they are solving the problems to make sure all their members know how to explain their answers.

When the dice are rolled, students must stop talking. The teacher calls out Group 5, person 2. Only person 2 responds:

> **Students as they interact with their peers take responsibility for their own learning.**

"We solved the equation as "...If the answer is right, the team scores a point. Mrs. Lopez adds Challenge problems to the strategy. She gives each team a challenging algebra problem to solve. For Challenge problems no dice are rolled. Any group may stand up and answer. Students receive three points for solving Challenge problems.

There are other formal cooperative strategies which like *Numbered Heads* engage students in learning. *Placemat Round Robin* can be used to get students to think about a topic of study.

Mr. Mike Warren uses the Numbered Heads cooperative strategy as an application or Apply activity in his history class. After the class has focused on the standard: *Analyze the historical development of Inventions after the Civil War,* Mr. Warren asks students in groups to think about how the inventions changed society. He then arranges students in groups of four. Each group is asked to draw a diagram like the one that follows on a large piece of butcher paper:

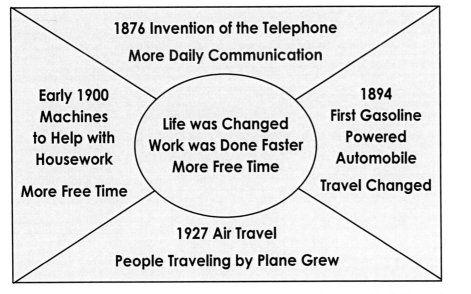

The outer spaces are used for each group to write their thoughts about the topic. A Round Robin is conducted to allow each group to share their views. The circle in the middle is used by groups to write their common conceptual understandings. Each group then reports to the class. This strategy encourages students to think about what they have learned and compare it to their peers' perspectives.

Student engagement cooperative strategies like *Numbered Heads, Challenge Numbered Heads* and *Placemat Round Robin* encourage students to apply content standards as they solve problems and reflect on what they have learned.

Allowing for Choice and Individual Goal Setting

The multidimensional approach is based on the premise that there are many ways to get to a standards-based learning goal. In this approach students are given the freedom to choose how they will acquire knowledge. While some students prefer to use linear text materials, others may become more engaged in learning through nonlinear internet sources. Still others may need visuals and audio renditions to learn. A hallmark of the multidimensional classroom is its flexibility. Students are encouraged by the teacher to problem solve and innovate.

The multidimensional approach is based on the premise that there are many ways to get to a standards-based learning goal. In this approach students are given the freedom to choose how they will acquire knowledge.

In contrast to the multidimensional perspective is the one-dimensional perspective. This perspective tells students not only what is to be learned but how it is to be learned. One-dimensional classrooms have a plethora of "must do" activities. Students are told the chapters to read and the questions to answer on any given topic. These structured activities leave little room for choice.

Mrs. Bertha Jones, a fifth grade teacher, approaches all learning in her classroom from a multidimensional perspective. She wants her students to learn subject matter and content standards but she believes there are many roads that lead to the same goal. Before starting an instructional unit, Mrs. Jones always tells students the standards to be mastered and the overall learning goal. She explains that the goal is to: Compare and contrast regions of the United States. She tells students the standards they are to master in the unit. These include the social studies standard: Students know the states located in the regions of the United States and the English language arts standards: Use correct capitalization of geographic names; Create simple documents using electronic media; and Understand how text features (diagrams, charts, maps) make information accessible and usable.

Mrs. Jones allows students to choose the geographic regions they want to research. Students establish their own learning goals. They choose whether they want to work alone, with a partner or in a group.

Mike writes the following learning goal: *I want to compare the commercial fishing industry in the region of New England to the Western region.* Mike chooses New England because his family is from Boston. Mike decides to work with a partner. They use the internet to gather statistics to compare and contrast commercial fishing in the two regions.

Sara and a team of students decide that their learning goal will be to compare and contrast the last 5 years' population growth in the Mid-Atlantic and Southwest regions. The team makes diagrams, graphs and charts to show their findings.

Another team of students decides to focus on the geographical similarities of the Southwest and the Midwest regions. They make a series of maps.

Mike and his teammates concentrate on identifying the major sources of revenue for the Great Plains region compared to the Southeast region. They complete spreadsheets documenting income streams.

All students master the overall standards-based learning goal established by the teacher. They accomplish this through a dynamic process of sharing, collaborating and interacting. This process facilitates students' learning concepts from multiple viewpoints and perspectives.

There are many similar assignments involving student choice that can be used for the upper elementary grades, middle school and high school. The 7th grade history standard: *Students analyze the geographic, political economic and religious and social structures of the civilizations of Medieval Europe* can be learned as students go back in time and choose a lifestyle for themselves by researching aspects of the political and social environment.

Life is about choices. This is especially true in the 21st century. Students will need to sift through an ever expanding number of facts to make choices to determine what information is important for decision making and problem solving.

Life is about choices. This is especially true in the 21st century. Students will need to sift through an ever expanding number of facts to make choices to determine what information is important for decision making and problem solving.

Student Engagement Strategies
Active Mastery of the Content Standards

The mastery of content standards is accelerated through the use of student engagement strategies. These activities give students the opportunity to reflect upon and apply the knowledge they have learned during the direct instruction or the *Teach part of the lesson.*

The *3-2-1* strategy can be used to find out what students have learned after a content lesson. At the end of a lesson, the teacher passes out index cards. The teacher has students write down three important terms or ideas to remember, two facts they would like to know more about and one concept, standard or skill they have mastered.

The mastery of content standards is accelerated through the use of student engagement strategies.

Mr. Rob Busto has taught the English language arts content standard: Articulate the relationship between the expressed purposes and the characteristics of different forms of literature (eg. comedy, tragedy) to his high school students. He implements the 3-2-1 strategy at the end of direct instruction. He passes out index cards to students. He asks students to write three important purposes of comedies and tragedies. Students then write two characteristics of these forms of literature that they would like to learn more about. Finally, they write one important characteristic of these forms of literature that they have mastered.

This strategy quickly gives the teacher an assessment on students' mastery of the structural features of literature. Students are given feedback as they share their *3-2-1* responses with a partner and the teacher.

When students get feedback, they are motivated to continue learning. This is especially true when it is positive, corrective, timely and targeted. Mr. Busto targets his immediate, corrective feedback to students' mastery of the content standard.

Other engagement strategies that target content mastery from elementary to high school include: *A Note to a Friend, Sort the Words* and *Ticket to Leave*.

The *Note to a Friend* engagement strategy helps students master a content standard by explaining it to a partner. Students have to think about what they have learned to teach it to someone else. Great explanations indicate that students have mastered the standard.

Mrs. Carol Seta uses the engagement strategy, A Note to a Friend after she has taught the 3rd grade math content standard: Know and understand that fractions and decimals are two representations of the same number. She has students write a Note to a Friend to explain how fractions and decimals can be used interchangeably.

The *Sort the Words* engagement strategy develops the important skill of categorization. Students sort words into conceptual groups.

Miss Silvia Sota has taught the English language arts standard: Capitalize Proper Nouns. She uses the student engagement strategy Sort the Words to provide students with the opportunity to process the standard they have just learned. She writes a number of words on the whiteboard. She has students sort out and capitalize the words that are proper nouns. Then as the students get ready to leave for recess, she uses the engagement strategy, Ticket to Leave. She passes out printed tickets the size of a half-sheet of paper. She has students write five proper nouns as their ticket to leave for recess.

The Ticket to Leave engagement strategy is particularly powerful at the end of the day. Students can sum up the standards they have learned.

The *Ticket to Leave* engagement strategy is particularly powerful at the end of the day. Students can sum up the standards they have learned. Oftentimes, students never think about the knowledge they have acquired. This strategy gives them the opportunity to reflect. It also gives the teacher feedback on what aspects of the standards taught were particularly relevant to students.

This strategy can be implemented anytime during the day. It can be used before students exit for recess or lunch. Students sum up what they have learned as their *Ticket to Leave* the classroom. The *Ticket to Leave* strategy reinforces the process of active reflection.

Engagement strategies that encourage the process of active reflection include: *Prediction Pairs, Graphic Summary, Mixed Up Summary, Review Partners, Inside-Outside Circles, Summing Up and Edit Response Groups.*

Prediction Pairs is an engagement strategy that reinforces the content standards and the creative thinking process. The skill of making predictions is an interdisciplinary skill that is targeted across content standards in language arts, math, science and history. The English language arts standard asks students to: *Make and confirm predictions about text by using prior knowledge.* In math, the standard requires students to: *Use prediction and estimation to verify the reasonableness of the calculated results.* The science standard states: *Predict the weather during a season by evaluating trends in temperature and rain.* The history standard is: *Predict historical events through past trends.* Predicting across subject areas engages students by having them make educated assumptions.

The engagement strategy entitled Prediction Pairs gives students practice in making assumptions or estimations. Making assumptions or estimations is a 21st century skill. As students make predictions they move from the known to the unknown.

Mrs. Lois Fair uses the strategy of Prediction Pairs as she targets the seventh grade English language arts standard: Analyze characterization as delineated through a character's thoughts and actions. As students are reading the literature selection, she has them predict in pairs what actions a character will take given what they have already read. Then she has students read to validate their predictions.

The engagement strategy entitled *Prediction Pairs* gives students practice in making assumptions or estimations. Making assumptions or estimations is a 21st century skill. As students make predictions they move from the known to the unknown. The teacher implements this strategy during the direct instruction part of the lesson. The teacher stops at strategic points and has students in pairs predict what will happen next. Predictions can be made by students after the teacher adds a new element to a science experiment or a new set of numerical data for problem solving in math. The strategy of "predicting" is learned best when it is used throughout the lesson or content unit.

Another active engagement strategy entitled *Graphic Summary* can be implemented across content areas after the direct instruction or *Teach* part of the lesson. Students are asked to summarize a content standard they have learned in a graphic summary.

Students may create a main idea webbed graphic, a Venn diagram or a pictorial representation. This strategy helps students master a content standard by putting it into a visual or graphic form.

After teaching the history standard: *Students analyze the political and social structures of Medieval Japan and China.* Mr. Adam Listo has students use a Venn diagram as a *Graphic Summary* to compare political structures. Pairs of students list the main elements of each country's political structures in the outside circles and their similarities where the circles intersect.

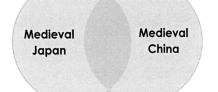

The *Mixed Up Summary* strategy engages students in organizing or reorganizing learned standards-based content information. Key content area vocabulary and concepts are written by the teacher in random order. Students individually or with a partner unscramble the content words and concepts and put them in the right sequential order. For Example, students can reorganize concepts they have learned mastering the science standard: *Energy and matter have multiple forms and can be changed from one form to another.* The *Mixed Up Summary* strategy like the *Graphic Summary* strategy engages students in the 21st century skill of transforming and synthesizing information.

Summing Up information is an important student engagement strategy that can be used across content disciplines. Reading across the curriculum necessitates comprehension of written and digital text. The teacher can quickly determine if students understand what they are reading by having them sum up a passage or a page.

Miss Julie Bowers is teaching the fifth grade standard: Discern main idea and concepts presented in texts. As students are reading their core language arts text, she has them stop after each page and summarize the main ideas by writing them as notes. English learners "sum up" information after each paragraph. The strategy of summing up short chunks of information increases comprehension.

> **The Mixed Up Summary strategy engages students in organizing or reorganizing learned standards-based content information.**

Students must use the higher level skill of synthesizing to "sum up' information. The skill of synthesizing is as valuable in science and history classes as it is in literature classes. Synthesizing is one of the most important skills for creativity.

Inside-Outside Circles is an engagement strategy that develops comprehension and the skill of synthesis. It is also a great way to review content vocabulary. The strategy is implemented as follows:

1. *Every student is given a flashcard with a question or a vocabulary term on it. Each student is required to answer the question or define the vocabulary word. Answers and definitions are checked by the teacher.*

2. Students line up. This can either be done randomly, according to height, length of name, etc. Then students count off in 2s.

3. The 1s are on the *outside* of the circle and the 2s are on the *inside* of the circle. The *outside* circle faces inward, while the *inside* circle faces outward. Each student numbered 1 faces a student numbered 2, as a partner.

4. Each pair reads the question on the other person's flash card and answers it. If the student misses the question, the person holding the card explains the answer.

5. After giving an appropriate amount of time to answer the questions, the teacher tells students on the *outside circle* to move in a clockwise direction. The *inside circle* remains where they are.

6. The process of answering questions and switching positions is repeated until the *outside* circle has gone around once.

7. Students on the *outside* and *inside* circles can switch cards, move one position and repeat the process again (Kagan, 1990).

This engagement strategy can be used across the curriculum. The geometry teacher can use it to review names of polygons or to review if-then statements. The English language arts teacher can review facts and opinions or vocabulary. The strategy can be utilized by a social studies or history teacher to review important events and their significance in changing the world.

> **The skill of synthesizing is as valuable in science and history classes as it is in literature classes. Synthesizing is one of the most important skills for creativity.**

All the above strategies engage students in the learning process. Research reveals that there is a significant correlation between high levels of engagement and mastery of subject content and standards (Brewster, 2000). Furthermore, engaged learners become Power Learners.

Games and Humor Support Power Learning

Power learning is supported by engagement strategies that include *games and humor*. The game *Twenty Questions* reinforces the standards in any content area. The teacher or students formulate twenty questions such as: *What numbers am I thinking about that are multiples of five? What are the ways energy can be transformed?* Humor also engages learners.

The *Silly Questions Game* asks students: *Can you think of twenty silly questions using synonyms for tiny?* Students like to laugh. Strategies that incorporate humor make students laugh and learn at the same time.

Higher Level Thinking and Power Learning

Engagement strategies that nurture *higher level thinking* facilitate Power Learning. Higher level thinking skills require students to analyze, synthesize and evaluate information. The *Best Practice* teacher asks inference questions across subject areas.

Mr. Nick Bennett's high school students are studying the concept of leadership in government. He is teaching the history standard: Understand the roles of United States government officials and elected leaders. He has students read several articles on influential government leaders. Then he asks students: What types of skills do these leaders have in common? What is the argument that would support the following claim: Leaders do not make good followers?

Mr. Bennett's questions require students to analyze and critique the articles they have read on government leaders. Students use critical and creative thinking to make inferences to answer the questions.

The teacher can encourage students to create their own higher level thinking questions before, during, or after a content unit of study. Students become engaged in learning by creating questions to: analyze information, evaluate alternatives, synthesize facts and create potential solutions for academic and social challenges.

Finally, engagement strategies hold all students responsible for their own learning. Power Learners are by definition self-directed learners. While most students can be motivated to become accountable for their own learning, there are still a number of students that remain disengaged and reluctant to participate in classroom activities. These students may need a more comprehensive accountability approach.

Accountability and Power Learning

One comprehensive student engagement model for reluctant middle school students is entitled the *Check and Connect Model* (Anderson et al., 2004). The model calls for the assignment of a monitor to each disengaged learner. The monitor first establishes a relationship or connects with the student. Then the monitor checks on the student's engagement by following up on school attendance and academic progress. The monitor uses individualized intervention strategies to help the disengaged student develop habits of Power Learning.

Best Practice student engagement strategies: *Support Content Standards Mastery, Activate Prior Knowledge, Foster Active Investigation, Promote Group Interaction, Encourage Collaboration, Allow for Choice, Include Games and Humor, Nurture Higher Level Thinking and Monitor Accountability.* The teacher uses these strategies to create active learners.

Active learners are interested in learning not to please the teacher, but to accomplish their own goals. Power Learners become independent thinkers.

Think About Discussion Questions

1. Choose one student engagement strategy on pages 116-117 that can be used to reinforce a content standard in the subject area you teach or in one of the subject areas you teach. Implement the strategy and write a reflection on the effectiveness of the strategy in helping students master the content standard.

2. Use the *3-2-1* student engagement strategy described on page 124 to review a lesson you have taught. Write a reflection on how well the strategy engaged students in your classroom.

Reflection on Power Learning and Student Engagement Strategies

1. What argument would you use to support or not support this claim: *The teacher sets the learning goals in the classroom. The students should be given the choice to decide how they will accomplish the goals?*

2. Reflect upon the learning activities in your classroom. On a scale of 1-10, rate the amount of time your students spend in cooperative discussion activities. Do you think student engagement would increase if students spent more time engaged in cooperative discussion?

Chapter 7

Engaging *Power Learners* Through Electronic Media

If you are planning for a year, sow rice; if you are planning for a decade, plant trees, if you are planning for a lifetime, educate people. (Chinese proverb)

We are no longer educating for a year, or even a decade, we are educating students for their lifetimes in the 21st century.

Everything in the 21st century is changing at an accelerated pace. The changes include: the way students access knowledge, the intensity of students' engagement with knowledge, the students' facilities with electronic media, and the students' abilities to multi-task knowledge streams. These 21st-century changes will accelerate the demand for knowledge that relies on an electronic network where media is varied in form and format (Treadwell, 2003).

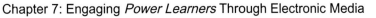

Creating 21st Century Power Learners

- *How do teachers facilitate the process of students becoming 21st century Power Learners?*

- *How is active learning facilitated through electronic media?*

- Why do WebQuests challenge students to direct their own learning?

- *How do WebQuests and Project-based assignments engage students in active, inquiry-based Power Learning?*

The focus for 21st century pedagogy is on facilitating the process for students to become knowledge networkers and innovators. The Best Practice teacher creates a 21st century information rich environment through the use of electronic media.

The creation of *Power Learners* that can function well in the 21st century global society requires a fundamental shift from 20th century text driven curriculum to 21st century pedagogy that emphasizes cyber-enabled information. Education in the 20th century was severely limited by the lack of an information rich knowledge network. Information was accessed through reading a limited collection of thematic books which were accorded Dewey decimal numbers. It was the librarian who managed information as she or he checked books in and out of the library (Treadwell, 2003).

Effective 21st century learning requires students to become the managers of information. They must learn how to bring together a collection of resources which are subsets of the internet. Students need to learn how to synthesize the information from the resources to create new understandings (Treadwell, 2003).

The focus for 21st century pedagogy is on facilitating the process for students to become knowledge networkers and innovators. The *Best Practice* teacher creates a 21st century information rich environment through the use of electronic media. The teacher has students use interactive technology to construct their own knowledge. Students, as they integrate information from multiple sources, learn to become intuitive. They use their intuition to select the right knowledge to answer content-based questions related to multidisciplinary problems and global challenges.

Students' selections of the "right facts" can no longer be done exclusively through text formats. This isn't because students can't gain knowledge or even become engaged in learning using text formats. It is because text formats can't build the knowledge network necessary for 21st century learning. Research confirms that multimedia formats empower learners to build knowledge more effectively (Treadwell, 2006). Technology gives students the opportunity to access information from all over the world.

Increasingly, 21st century knowledge building pedagogy is being created in web formats and stored on worldwide databases. These Web formats no longer require content units to be paper-based. Content units can be composed of multimedia elements containing flexible options. Multimedia content units engage students through interactive, multimodality learning. Students build their understanding of concepts through rich information and communication sources.

Multimedia Web Formats

Multimedia formats are more stimulating and engaging for students at all ages. Many of the problems schools are experiencing with disengaged learners, especially at the middle school and high school levels, result from the disconnect that exists between the outside technological world with all its visual and auditory stimuli, and the often static classroom environments. Students in these classrooms are inundated with hours of lecture-based direct instruction.

WebQuests use authentic tasks to engage students in the learning process. The activities on WebQuests are designed around Best Practices in teaching.

Lectures no matter how good they are, do not sustain student interest for long. Web applications like WebQuests, however, have the potential to capture students' attention for hours. WebQuests engage students in actively applying content information, rather than passively listening. Students apply knowledge through inquiry-based activities.

WebQuests use authentic tasks to engage students in the learning process. The activities on WebQuests are designed around *Best Practices* in teaching.

March defines the purpose and advantages of WebQuests in the following quote:

Webquests are scaffolded learning structures that use links to essential resources on the World Wide Web. They use authentic tasks to engage students in the investigation of a central, open-ended question. They develop students' individual research expertise. WebQuests also motivate students to transform newly acquired information into more sophisticated understandings. The best WebQuests inspire students to see rich thematic relationships, make real world connections, and reflect on their own metacognitive processes (March, 2006).

WebQuests Engage Students in 21ˢᵗ Century Learning

WebQuests include the research-based Best Practice student engagement strategies of: *scaffolding knowledge, focusing on constructivist learning, integrating inference questions, making thematic connections and using authentic assessment.*

Research indicates that student achievement accelerates when scaffolds or temporary frameworks are used to support student performance beyond their current level (Cho, 2004). WebQuests engage students by dividing learning activities into manageable tasks and directing students' attention to specific goals (Ngeow, 2001). Learning tasks in WebQuests are scaffolded one upon another so that students can move easily from a simple to a more complex level of learning.

WebQuests use authentic tasks. *Authentic learning* is a Best Practice for student engagement. John Keller's ARCS model for student engagement fits well with WebQuest learning. WebQuest activities capture students' *Attention*, are *Relevant* to their needs, give students the *Confidence* it takes for achievement and ultimately give learners the *Satisfaction* of their accomplishments.

The best WebQuests inspire students to see rich thematic relationships, make real world connections, and reflect on their own metacognitive processes.

Constructivist Learning

WebQuests use a constructivist approach to learning. Students engage in authentic tasks to answer open-ended questions. *Constructivist learning* is a Best Practice engagement strategy that creates high achievers. Early constructivists did research that confirmed that "Puzzlement is the factor that engages students in learning" (Savery and Duffy, 1995).

WebQuests engage students by building on prior knowledge and allowing students to transform what they have learned into new understandings. Some WebQuests go so far as to pose contradictions. Other WebQuests engage students in research inquiries that are designed to challenge and transform students' current beliefs.

Students transform information in WebQuests by responding to higher level thinking questions that require them to synthesize facts and concepts in an innovative way. The goal is for students to create something substantively different from the knowledge that already exists. This means that their creation must be more than a new compilation of unprocessed facts.

WebQuests engage students by building on prior knowledge and allowing students to transform what they have learned into new understandings.

Bransford (2005) discusses this concept of transformation in learning by distinguishing between the activation of pre-existing knowledge and the development of new knowledge and skills. His research suggests that teachers provide learners with problem-solving activities that include critical thinking to support schema construction.

For example, a WebQuest on learning about the fifty states would include active schema creation and transformative learning by having students as a group respond to the following open-ended question: *Based on its natural resources, social policies, main businesses, climate, and history, which state of those you've studied is most likely to be successful in the later 21st century? Decide what criteria you will use to define and evaluate what it means for a state to be "successful."* This task requires students to use the information they have learned in a new way to construct deeper understandings and to create new paradigms (March, 2006).

Cooperative Power Learning

The creation of new paradigms is facilitated by the cooperative learning that WebQuests foster. Students work together on WebQuests to answer open-ended questions like: *How can you use what you know about the Amazon rainforest to provide a solution to what should be done to save this endangered habitat?*

Cooperative learning is tied to themes in WebQuests. *Thematic activities* are used to engage students in interdisciplinary learning. A substantial research base supports thematic teaching because it helps students make logical connections among disciplines. This increases the opportunity for students to transfer learning from one context to another (Kagan,1990).

WebQuests promote students' transfer of learning through the 21st century skill of conducting interdisciplinary research. Inquiry-based WebQuests extend the learning in core subject texts. Web-based activities are interactive and media-rich. They are tied to varied perspectives. Typically, students participating in a WebQuest assume different roles. This allows a team of learners to investigate an issue from multiple viewpoints as represented by a sub-set of Web sites. As students integrate perspectives they construct multidimensional interpretations of information.

Authentic Assessment

The Best Practice of authentic assessment is used in WebQuests. Students evaluate their own learning as individuals and as members of learning teams. Research shows that self and group assessment engages students (Hattie, 2002). Learners test their newly constructed knowledge against the feedback of their peers.

Authentic assessment as self-evaluation is done by students on rubrics. A rubric is a scoring tool that lists the criteria for a piece of work (Perkins, 2006). For example, students may be evaluated on organization, details, voice and mechanics. Assessment on rubrics also articulates gradations of quality for each criterion from excellent to poor.

A self-evaluation rubric for elementary school students usually contains the following elements: group participation, on task behavior and a grammar component focusing on capitalization and punctuation. Middle school and high school students can evaluate themselves on group effort, content and on written conceptual delivery. Evaluations for high school students may include a continuum with categories such as: beginning, developing, superior and exemplary.

The following rubric was created to evaluate students' reports describing their creative inventions. It lists the criteria and gradations of quality for written, verbal or graphic reports. The rubric is effective in evaluating reports on all students' inventions which may range from new transportation vehicles to mechanisms that prevent pollution (Perkins, 2006).

The four columns on the following rubric describe the varying degrees of quality, from excellent to poor. They explain what makes a report acceptable or not acceptable.

RUBRIC FOR AN INVENTION REPORT				
Criteria	**Quality**			
Purposes	The report explains all the key purposes of the invention.	The report explains some of the purposes.	The report misses key purposes.	The report does not refer to the purposes.
Features	The report explains the majority of features.	The report details key and hidden features.	The report neglects some features.	The report does not detail the features.
Critique	The report discusses the strengths and weaknesses of the invention and suggests improvements	The report discusses some of the strengths and weaknesses of the invention.	The report discusses either the strengths or weaknesses of the invention but not both.	The report does not mention the strengths or the weaknesses of the invention.
Connect	The report makes appropriate connections between the purposes and features of the invention.	The report makes some connections between the purposes and features of the invention.	The report makes unclear or inappropriate connections between purposes of the invention.	The report makes no connections between the invention and other things.

(Adapted from Perkins, 1994)

WebQuests and Active Standards-Based Learning

The *Best Practice* teacher can design his or her own WebQuests or use WebQuests that have already been developed. There are a number of WebQuest development sites that take teachers through the process of WebQuest design. WebQuests normally have the following components: *Introduction, Task, Process, Evaluation and Conclusion.*

> *Ms. Mary Carlyle is finishing a literature unit with the theme of respect with her third grade class. She searches the Internet for elementary WebQuests to end the unit. She finds a WebQuest entitled: A Quest for Respect with the Grouchy Ladybug (Frey, Meinholtz, Reed, 2006). She decides to adapt the WebQuest for her students.*

> *Ms. Carlyle introduces the WebQuest by reading her class the book, The Grouchy Ladybug by Eric Carle. She then gives students an oral Introduction on the purpose of the WebQuest. She defines for students the Task. She walks students through the Process they will use to complete the task. Finally, she gives students the Evaluation criteria.*

The WebQuest that Ms. Carlyle uses for her third graders is organized around learning tasks and processes. Before laying out the tasks and processes, she gives students an introduction to what they are going to learn.

The following is an outline of Ms. Carlyle's presentation of the WebQuest entitled the *Grouchy Ladybug* (adapted from Frey, Meinholz and Reed, 2006). This is an example of a WebQuest that can be used at the early elementary levels.

WebQuest Learning Tasks and Processes

Introduction: *This story tells you about a grouchy ladybug that disrespects and is mean to everyone she meets. At the end of the story she finally learns good manners and how to respect others. What does it mean to respect others?*

You are going to do a WebQuest to discover the many meanings of respect. You are also going to become a ladybug expert.

Task: *Reread the book, <u>The Grouchy Ladybug</u> to a partner. Then work with your partner to complete the following tasks: 1) Chart the activities of the grouchy ladybug that show disrespect. 2) Chart the activities that show respect. 3) Write your own meaning of respect. 4) Draw a picture of what respect means to you. 5) Research facts about real ladybugs. (Ms. Carlyle also includes links as resources including one that defines respect and another that gives facts about ladybugs).*

Process: *Follow these steps to complete the WebQuest:*

1) *Read <u>The Grouchy Ladybug</u> to a partner.*

2) *Make a chart with a partner like the one below. Describe the activities of the grouchy ladybug that showed her meanness and disrespect for others. Give an accounting of her activities every hour.*

5:00 A.M. The grouchy ladybug didn't want to share, so she flew away.
6:00 A.M. The grouchy ladybug tried to fight with the yellow jacket. Etc.
7:00 A.M.

3) *Look up the meaning of respect by clicking on the word.*

4) *Research real ladybugs. Click on the picture of the ladybug. Write five facts about ladybugs in sentences.*

5) *Follow the directions to draw your own ladybug with a partner.*

6) *Discuss with a partner what you learned about feelings and respect. Act out with a partner what the story characters would say to the grouchy ladybug about respecting the feelings of others.*

WebQuest Evaluation Rubrics

Evaluation: *Your work will be checked on a teacher and student rubric.*

Student Rubric	Yes	No
I helped my partner.		
I listened to my partner's ideas.		
I did my best.		

Teacher Rubric	1 Point	2 Points
Participation	Partners participate.	Partners cooperate.
Thinking Process	Partners on task.	Partners verbalize what is learned.
Writing Process	Complete written activities.	Use complete sentences.

(adapted from Frey, Meinholz and Reed, 2006)

Conclusion: *You are now a respectful ladybug expert.*

Third graders in Ms. Carlyle's class became actively involved with the book, *The Grouchy Ladybug,* through this WebQuest. Students discovered more about the meaning of respect from the WebQuest than they could ever have learned from just the passive reading of the book. Students worked together to find information. At the end of the WebQuest, students were evaluated on the effectiveness of their collaboration.

The Grouchy Ladybug WebQuest Ms. Carlyle used followed the format used by most WebQuests. The *Introduction* sets the stage for learning. Ms. Carlyle used the introduction to orally tell students the purpose of the WebQuest. Oftentimes, a WebQuest may start with a short paragraph to introduce the purpose of the activity. Ms. Carlyle laid out what she wanted students to accomplish in the *Task.* The *Task* included interactive activities including: charting, discussing and finding information with a partner.

Other *Tasks* on WebQuests may include: solving a problem, defending a position, designing a product, or creating a story. The task is anything that requires students to transform the information they have gathered. Ms. Carlyle created the directions in the Process part of the WebQuest to facilitate students' reorganization and transformation of their ideas into a chart format.

Reorganizing and Transforming Information

Reorganizing and transforming information is an integral part of WebQuests and also an important 21st century skill for Power Learning. Students can reorganize information on flow charts or graphic organizers. The Process component may suggest a checklist of questions for students to analyze and think about. Students may also be linked to "E sheets or prepared guide documents."

Ms. Carlyle used a Self Assessment and a Teacher Assessment Rubric as authentic evaluations of students' learning tasks. Rubrics are the preferred way to evaluate the understandings students acquired from WebQuests.

Self assessment is part of the process of helping students become self motivated learners. A number of rubrics can be reviewed on these sites: *Rubrics http://www.edb.utexas. edu/projects/allen/rubric.html and http://edweb.sdsu/ triton/july/rubrics/Rubrics for WebLessons.html. (valid at printing.)*

Finally, the WebQuest Ms. Carlyle used had a *Conclusion.* The Conclusion summarizes in one sentence what students have learned by completing the WebQuest. Ms. Carlyle summarized the learning for her students by stating: *You now have become respectful ladybug experts.* The conclusion of a WebQuest often includes extension questions or additional links to encourage critical and creative thinking.

Additional links for the WebQuest could include links to other books with the theme of respect. Links could also be related to similar themes like kindness and perseverance. When WebQuests are used along with text materials, students learn to apply reading skills to digital formats.

> *Reorganizing and transforming information is an important part of WebQuests and also an important 21st century skill for Power Learning.*

WebQuests and Multicultural Learning

WebQuests are powerful tools for interdisciplinary and multicultural learning. Students can become immersed in cultural customs and events of cultural significance. The following WebQuest on Cinco de Mayo engages students in finding information about this historical event. Students also listen to culturally relevant literature and music. The task is laid out as follows:

Task: *The newspaper reporter for community events is out of town. Our class is going to take his place as reporters to cover events for Cinco de Mayo. You will gather information about Cinco de Mayo and then give your own interpretation why the day is important in the Mexican culture. You must research literature on Cinco de Mayo and listen to culturally relevant music. You can click on the chili peppers on the WebQuest to get links to additional information on Cinco de Mayo. Be sure to explain the difference between Cinco de Mayo and Mexican Independence Day* (adapted from Cox, 2008).

This task actively engages students in a cultural learning experience. Students become immersed in the literature and music which relates to this historical event. The goal of the Cinco de Mayo WebQuest is for students to transform the cultural information they acquire into their own interpretation of the holiday's meaning. As students recreate and interpret information for themselves, they begin to become self-directed learners.

WebQuests for Middle School and High School

WebQuests that facilitate information transformation are especially valuable at the middle school and high school levels. WebQuests at these levels can cover any subject content area. The best WebQuests for middle school and high school students use a multidisciplinary approach to learning. They require students to use English language arts, math, history and science standards. One exciting multidisciplinary WebQuest for high school students is based on the novel, *Anthem* by Ayn Rand. The *Task* for students is to first read the book. Then students work in cooperative learning groups to design a *Utopian Society* (adapted from Good, 2006).

Besides great visuals, the *Utopian Society* WebQuest has engaging multidisciplinary standard-based learning activities. It begins with the teacher explaining the content area standards that are integral to the WebQuest. These include: the English language arts standard: *Write a persuasive essay;* the math standard: *Describe geometric objects;* the science standard: *Evaluate the accuracy and reproducibility of data;* and the history standard: *Identify systems of government.*

The *Introduction* engages students by using a quote from the book, *Anthem* by Ayn Rand. It also sets the stage for the group challenge of creating a utopian society (adapted from Good, 2006).

Introduction: *"It is a sin to write this. It is a sin to think words no others think and to put them down upon paper no others see."* Prometheus and Gaea have begun the new age of reasoning. As their children, you have the task of designing the new world order. It is up to you to create the utopian society (Good, 2006).

The *Task* is to create a utopian society. The *Process* for accomplishing this task engages students in cooperative group learning. The group must decide who will take the roles of scientist, philosopher, historian and human rights activist. Each role has a research link with questions that need to be answered. For example, one question for the scientist is: *What are the most important future technologies/scientific advances that your utopian society should include?* Students answer questions by using electronic resources and by referring to the book, *Anthem* by Ayn Rand.

> **The best WebQuests for middle school and high school students use a multidisciplinary approach to learning. They require students to use English language arts, math, history and science standards.**

Students as scientists, historians and philosophers present their research and conclusions at a group meeting. The historians relate what they learned about the positive and negative aspects of current governments around the world. The scientists discuss how technological inventions have changed societies and how they will change societies in the future. The philosophers discuss the ethics of creating a utopian society. This information is used as background knowledge for the group to take what was learned and transform it into a utopian society for the future.

Students use the process of consensus building to decide on the optimum government model. After students have created the model, they write a persuasive essay to persuade others to adopt their model.

> *Activities in the WebQuest are scaffolded. They build on students' understandings of government models. Students transform this knowledge by using applied imagination to create a utopian society.*

Each student writes the essay from the perspective of his or her role as scientist, philosopher, human rights activist or historian. After writing the essay, students develop a three dimensional physical model of their utopian society. The design of the model reflects unique aspects of the futuristic society.

The *Evaluation* component includes a teacher and student rubric. Rubrics evaluate student performance on: *content, group effort, individual essays and the physical model.* The categories for evaluation are: beginning, developing, accomplished and exemplary (Good, 2006).

Student Engagement Strategies Facilitate Power Learning

The Utopian Society WebQuest uses all the student engagement strategies that facilitate Power Learning. These include: *scaffolding knowledge, using a constructivist approach to learning, using inference questions, using thematic activities and using authentic assessment.* The WebQuest has the added instructional advantage of using interdisciplinary learning and standard-based instruction.

Activities in the WebQuest are scaffolded. They build on students' understandings of government models. Students transform this knowledge by using applied imagination to create a utopian society.

Higher level thinking questions are asked and answered as students analyze, evaluate and synthesize facts to develop concepts. The Utopian Society WebQuest uses a thematic approach to engage students in the process of creating a new society. Finally, students use an authentic assessment.

WebQuests such as the ones described in this chapter use Best Practice student engagement strategies to create inquiry-oriented lessons. Students use WebQuests to transform information into new understandings and creations.

Project-based Learning

Project-based Learning is a multimedia approach that can be used along with WebQuests to facilitate active Power Learning. The best types of projects are constructivist-based and applicable to real-world issues (Dodge, 2001).

This type of learning like WebQuests is multidisciplinary. Students apply content standards throughout their project-based research to transform knowledge and create new paradigms. They apply these new paradigms by making academic, global and social connections.

Mr. Bud Borgos has designed a Project-based lesson for his eighth grade students to carry out over the next month. He builds into the project a number of subject area standards including: the English language arts standard: Uses proposition and support patterns; the history standard; Understands changing world views; the science standard: Construct appropriate graphs from data and develop quantitative statements; and the math standard: Uses nonstandard units to describe the measurements of objects.

> ***Students apply content standards throughout their project-based research to transform knowledge and create new paradigms. They apply these new paradigms by making academic, global and social connections.***

Mr. Borgos selects the theme Future Inventions for a Technological World to correlate with the history core text reading on the influence of technology in a changing society. Mr. Borgos assigns students to four groups. Each group is asked to select one of four ideas for future technological inventions that could change society. These ideas for future technological inventions include: free energy, a transporter using a person's atoms, a replicator for technology, and a universal communicator.

He directs students to choose one of four roles: efficiency expert, scientist, communicator or illustrator. Students are given the task of integrating a number of multimedia applications to find information on the concept of their chosen invention from the standpoint of their roles. After students share information with their group, they collaborate to create one of the future technological inventions. Students are to frame in writing the proposition and support patterns used for their creation. They are to design their invention using nonstandard units of measurement. Finally, they are to self-assess their learning both as individuals and as group members on an authentic assessment rubric. Mr. Borgos will use the same rubric to assess students.

The eight elements of project-based learning include: standards-based curricular content, multimedia, student decision making, collaborative group work, global connections, multidisciplinary learning, authentic assessment and an extended time frame.

Mr. Bud Borgos uses the eight elements of project-based learning to engage his eighth grade students. These elements include: standards-based curricular content, multimedia, student decision making, collaborative group work, global connections, multidisciplinary learning, authentic assessment and an extended time frame. He engages students in Power Learning as they move from what exists to what could be.

Students collaborate and make decisions on how to construct the technological invention for the future. They use multidisciplinary research to support their thinking. They make global connections on how the technology will change society for the better. They continue to work on the invention throughout the extended time frame Mr. Burgos has given them to complete the project.

WebQuests and Project-based Learning 21st Century Pedagogies

WebQuests and Project-based learning are two powerful ways to engage students. Both pedagogies motivate students by using 21st century multimedia and authentic learning situations that are based on the content standards. These learning approaches facilitate the active Power Learning process.

The *Best Practice* teacher has an important role as the facilitator of 21st century learning. As facilitator, the teacher designs authentic learning experiences for students. Then he or she steps back and lets students direct their own learning. As students take on learning tasks, they utilize higher level thinking to find answers and solutions to global challenges. Students apply and synthesize their new understandings in WebQuests or Project-based learning. They discover multidisciplinary connections. They begin to see learning as a constructivist activity. They get excited as they find information to support their theories. Students no longer need prodding by the teacher. They are self-motivated.

WebQuests and Project-based learning most importantly engage students in applying the 21st century skills of: working with others, synthesizing facts for decision making and using applied imagination to solve complex real life challenges. These are the 21st century skills that students need for academics and for their future careers.

Think About Discussion Questions

1. Find one WebQuest on the Internet that complements the content standards you are teaching. Write a reflection on how students can use this WebQuest to interact with sources on the Internet and transform knowledge.

2. Create an evaluation rubric for a standards-based WebQuest that students in your class can implement at the end of a lesson.

Reflection on Engaging Learners Through Electronic Media

1. Reflect on the limitations of using only text-based materials in the classroom. How would you evaluate the transferability of learning to an increasingly technology-driven 21st century world?

2. Reflect on how you would create a Project-based learning lesson for the content area you teach. Create a theme-based outline that includes some of your content standards.

Chapter 8

Summary of Student Engagement Strategies

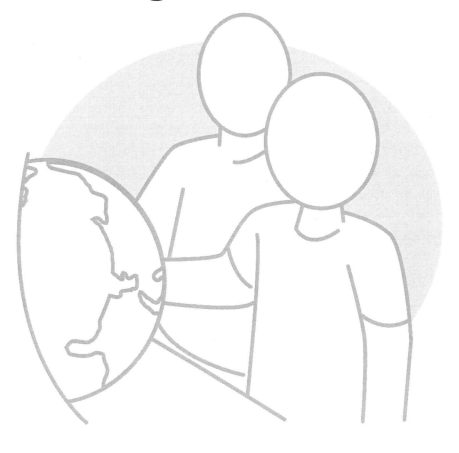

Research shows that students who are engaged in active learning retain knowledge better. Best Practice teachers systematically implement student engagement strategies prepare students to participate in the team driven global interconnected workforce.

Now that you've learned how student engagement and motivation are intricately tied to the learning process, you may want to use extrinsic learning reinforcers to increase students' on task classroom behaviors. Extrinsic behavioral reinforcers are: *raising students' level of concern, using feeling tones, praising students' success, engaging students' interest and giving students knowledge of results* (Hunter, 2004). You may want to stand next to disengaged learners to raise their *level of concern*. When you see students on task, you can build on positive *feeling tones* by using *The Power of Praise*. Praise is most effective when it focuses on students' making an effort, no matter how small.

> **Now that you've learned how student engagement and motivation are intricately tied to the learning process, you may want to use extrinsic learning reinforcers to increase students on task classroom behaviors.**

Focus upon the statement: *Nothing succeeds like success*. Students are more motivated when they succeed at learning.

They are more motivated when they get answers right, rather than wrong. You may want to implement the simple extrinsic motivation strategy of having students circle their right answers, rather than their wrong answers. Remember also that *success* is most powerful as a motivator when students have to put forth effort to create the success. Think about how you can differentiate instruction by designing learning tasks where students need to put forth effort, but the end result of the effort is success. Don't forget as you're creating these activities to chunk them down for English language learners taking into consideration their motivational styles.

Along with creating the opportunities for students to be successful in learning, you may want to think about the power of *interest* in motivating students. Students learn what interests them. Determine how you can create active learning activities that capture students' interests and imaginations. Finally, don't forget the last powerful extrinsic motivator: *knowledge of results*. Giving students immediate feedback on what they need to do to improve their work has a significant effect not only on students' motivations but also on their achievements.

After you have thought about how you will extrinsically motivate students, your next goal is to facilitate the process whereby students become self-motivated or intrinsically motivated to learn. Reflect upon the Best Practice strategies that increase students' intrinsic motivation in instructional settings.

These include the *10 C's of Motivation: Confidence, Choice, Content Integration, Challenge, Command, Collaboration, Conversation, Constructivism, Creation and Celebration.*

Consider the student engagement strategies that encourage students to become self motivated or *Power Learners.* You may choose to implement student engagement strategies like *Think-Pair-Share, Jigsaw, Whiteboarding and Brainstorming* in your daily activities. There are a number of student engagement strategies in this book that you may apply in your classroom to facilitate *Power Learning.*

These include strategies that: *activate prior knowledge, (KWL)* promote group interaction *(Cooperative Learning),* encourage collaboration *(Multiple Solutions),* allow for choice *(Jet Setting Pets),* include games and humor *(20 Silly Questions),* support content skills mastery *(Prediction Pairs),* nurture higher level thinking *(Open-ended Questioning)* and monitor student accountability *(Check and Connect Model).*

Finally, students who will spend their lives in the 21st century need access to electronic media for learning. Think about how you can create *Power Learners* by engaging students in activities which require them to manage and transform information. Best Practices for the 21st century include using technology rich information environments where students can construct their own knowledge. Some of the best learning activities are continually being created in Web formats and stored on worldwide data bases. Analyze how you can deliver content instruction that moves away from paper-based learning and moves toward multimedia units containing flexible options for students. Remember that lectures, no matter how exciting you make them, can only sustain student interest for so long. Think about how you can follow up your direct instruction with *WebQuests* and *Project-based learning.* These pedagogies use *Best Practice* strategies to create active *Power Learning* scenarios.

It is really through your motivating and engaging students in active learning that they begin to want to learn not only to please you but to please themselves. As you see students in your class become self motivated Power Learners, you can be assured that you are a highly successful facilitator of the learning process.

> **Think about how you can create Power Learners by engaging students in activities which require them to manage and transform information.**

Student Engagement Strategies and Power Learning

Student engagement strategies that facilitate Power Learning or active self-directed learning:

❖ *involve students in the learning process*

❖ *utilize cooperative discussion*

❖ *activate prior knowledge*

❖ *foster active imagination*

❖ *promote group interaction*

❖ *encourage collaboration*

❖ *allow for choice*

❖ *include games and humor*

❖ *support content standards mastery*

❖ *nurture higher level thinking skills*

❖ *monitor student accountability*

❖ *use interactive electronic media*

❖ *use project-based multidisciplinary learning*

Strategies that Involve Students in the Learning Process

❖ Quick Writes

A *quick write* can be solicited at the beginning, in the middle, or at the end of a content unit. At the beginning of a unit the *quick write* prompt may be an open-ended question that enables the teacher to find out what students know about a topic. Students may use *quick writes* in the middle of a unit to list their questions about a topic. The conclusion of a unit may use a *quick write* prompt to have students summarize what they have learned.

> A *quick write* prompt that can be used to start a unit on geography is: *Write the names of the seven continents and something you know about each continent.*

> A *quick write* prompt to end an earth science unit is: *Explain or illustrate how the moon's appearance changes during the four-week lunar cycle.*

❖ Physical Responses

Teachers make a statement and students respond with *thumbs up* (agree), *thumbs down* (disagree), *thumbs to the side* (unsure).

Students can also use agreed upon *hand motions* like moving *a hand up and down for yes* and *sideways for no.*

❖ Physical Movements

Brain research states that the more students are active in the learning process, the more they learn. *Physical movements* like standing up and giving choral answers help students learn and retain information. Snapping or clapping out letters in spelling words using the *Rule of 3* helps students with comprehension and spelling.

❖ Response Cards

Students hold up *response cards* to answer the teacher's queries. Response cards are two-sided.

One side can say *yes.* The other side can say *no.*

The teacher might ask: *Are there seven continents in the world?*

Students hold up yes or no. This gives the teacher immediate feedback on what students know.

The teacher can use *two-sided cards* to engage students in any multidisciplinary learning activity. Students can hold up cards that say:

> *agree/disagree*
> *right/wrong*
> *correct/incorrect*
> *valid/invalid*
> *noun/verb*
> *simple sentence/compound sentence*
> *fact/opinion*
> *add/subtract*
> *complete sentence/incomplete sentence*

❖ *Learning by Doing*

Researchers have documented that students retain only 5% of the information they hear through a lecture. They retain 95% of the information they learn when they are actively engaged in constructing knowledge.

Constructivist learning involves students in utilizing knowledge as they experience it, evaluate it, and attempt to make sense out of it using their prior knowledge.

Students as they construct their own knowledge engage in: wondering, questioning, forming hypotheses, communicating and investigating.

Constructivist activities include: multidisciplinary research projects, role playing (taking on the roles of doctors or scientists when studying the human body), experiments, and group problem solving.

Data driven dialogue and purposeful conversations accelerate the learning of English for English language learners. Purposeful dialogue is defined as conversations that relate to problem solving or finding information to complete a research assignment. As English language learners interact with peers, they learn vocabulary and language patterns.

Student Engagement
Cooperative Discussion Strategies

❖ Think-Pair-Share

Think-Pair-Share is a Best Practice Cooperative Discussion strategy that promotes active learning. Instead of listening passively to a lecture, students actively share their thoughts about what they are learning with a partner.

The *Think-Pair-Share* process begins with the teacher posing a challenging or *open-ended* question. Students are given time to think about the question and then time to share their responses with a partner.

The *Think-Pair-Share* strategy has four steps. Each step has a time limit signaled by the teacher.

- **Step One:** The teacher asks an *open-ended* question where there is no right answer.

- **Step Two:** Students think individually. This is the *Think* part of the *Think-Pair-Share*. Students are given one to two minutes to think about their answers. The teacher uses a signal to indicate time is up.

- **Step Three:** Students discuss their answers with a partner. This is the *Pair-Share* part of the *Think-Pair-Share*. The *Pair-Share* gives students the opportunity to try out their answers on partners before sharing them with the class.

- **Step Four:** Students share their answers with the class. This is the *Share* part of the *Think-Pair-Share* strategy (Lyman, 1987, Vaca, 2002).

❖ *Jigsaw Cooperative Discussion Strategy*

The jigsaw was developed as a group discussion technique (Aronson, 2006). The idea is analogous to a jigsaw puzzle. Students do research on a subject topic in groups. Each person in the group researches one aspect or piece of the topic. Then informational pieces are put together in the form of peer teaching. Each person in the group teaches his fellow students the facts related to the subtopic he or she has researched. Just as in a jigsaw, each piece of information is essential for full understanding of the topic.

How to Set Up a Class Jigsaw

1. Divide the class into four or five teams. Assign each group member a part of the topic or subtopic.

2. Members of teams with the same subtopic meet together in expert groups. A variety of research materials, as well as the internet are made available to expert groups. Expert groups use these resources to find information about their subtopic.

3. Experts return to jigsaw teams to teach what they have learned to peers.

4. Team members listen and take notes on the information taught by peers.

5. Students write a group report integrating the pieces of information they have learned from all the experts. Students can also be given a test on the topic (Rudell, 2003).

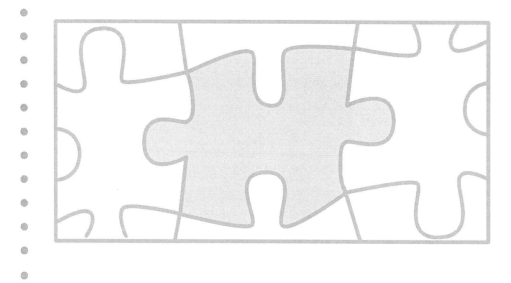

❖ *Brainstorming*

The technique of *Brainstorming* promotes the thinking process without restrictions. This means there are no right or wrong answers. Brainstorming encourages "wild ideas." Judgment of ideas is withheld. Students are encouraged to piggyback on the ideas of others.

The purpose of Brainstorming is to focus student attention on the process of idea generation. This process is important prior to beginning writing or problem solving.

Brainstorming that focuses on applied imagination is a 21st century skill.

Questions for Brainstorming are open-ended. Examples of open-ended questions that can be used for *Brainstorming* are:

- *What if everything in the world was green?*

- *What would have happened if the United States had not entered World War II?*

- *What other uses can there be for a felt hat other than a head covering?*

- *What are three new inventions that would be most useful to the world?*

- *How would you improve the cafeteria food?*

❖ *Whiteboards and Student Engagement*

Whiteboards are the 21st century version of the chalk slates used by students in colonial times. They provide a great way of engaging students in active learning. Whiteboards are a terrific tool for immediate feedback and assessment.

Whiteboards facilitate and support a 21st century constructivist approach to learning. Students use whiteboards as tools for creation.

Whiteboards can be used from elementary to high school to engage students in learning. These are some uses of whiteboards.

- Math: Students write answers to teacher-posed math problems on a whiteboard. Students can also solve a problem by making a chart or visual on the whiteboard.

- Writing: Students can brainstorm ideas with a partner on a whiteboard.

- English Language Arts: Students do quick writes on a whiteboard.

- English language learners can use whiteboards to write sentences. Answers on whiteboards are easily corrected.

- Spelling: One student dictates words. The other student writes the words on the whiteboard.

- Social Studies/Science. Large whiteboards are used for brainstorming or recording facts and concepts.

Student Engagement Strategies that Activate Prior Knowledge and Understandings

❖ **KWL** is a classic student engagement strategy that activates prior knowledge. The teacher starts the lesson by having students write what they know about a topic. Then the students write what they want to know. Finally, at the end of the lesson students write what they have learned. (5-10 minutes)

❖ **KWL Pairs** begins by having students brainstorm in writing what they *Know* about a topic. Students then formulate written questions about what they *Wonder* about. After the teacher's direct instruction on the topic, student pairs circle the known information that was covered. They put asterisks next to questions that were answered and summarize the other facts and concepts they have *Learned*. (5 minutes)

❖ **Roundtable** begins by the teacher asking an open ended question. The teacher then puts students in groups. The teacher gives each group a sheet of paper. Each student in the group writes an answer to the teacher's question and then passes the sheet to the person on his or her left. Students discuss their answers. (10-15 minutes)

❖ **Webbing** has students in partners organize what they know about a topic in the form of a graphic organizer. Students put the topic in the center and what they know around it. They can later fill in the web with items they have learned. (10-15 minutes)

Student Engagement Active Investigation Strategies

❖ **Multiple Solutions** motivates students to come up with alternative answers to questions or problems. The teacher can prompt student critical thinking by posing questions or problems that are open-ended and have no one right answer. Examples of questions that inspire students to come up with multiple answers include: *How many ways can you sort these green plants? How many equations can you write to solve the problem? Who has a different idea for the solution to this problem?* (5 minutes)

❖ **Detective** engages students in the study of a new topic. The primary purpose of this strategy is to have students begin study on a new topic by doing research. For example, a history lesson on the Causes of World War II instead of commencing with having students read a text chapter, would have students become *detectives*. Students as detectives find information about World War II. (15-20 minutes)

❖ **RoundAbout** is a strategy for involving students in thinking about a topic and then doing research. The strategy begins by putting students in teams. The teacher then poses a topic for study. Using a sheet of paper, students make a list of what they want to find out about the topic. Each person on the team writes a question for research and then passes it to the next student on the team. The Roundabout strategy gives all team members the opportunity to give alternative ideas for topic study. (10-20 minutes)

❖ **Four Corners** is a student engagement strategy that is especially effective when students are studying a controversial or thought provoking topic. The teacher begins the Four Corners strategy by posing a situation or dilemma. The teacher then asks students to go to one of four corners of the room which are marked *Strongly Agree, Agree, Strongly Disagree and Disagree*. Students in each group exchange their opinions. They summarize their reasoning on a large whiteboard or chart paper. They share their thinking with the class. (15-20 minutes)

❖ **Send a Question or Problem** is a consensus building strategy. The teacher implements this strategy by first arranging students in teams. Students on each team are asked to create a question or a problem relating to a topic of study or a content standard. Questions or problems are written on index cards. Students on one team pass their cards to students on another team. Students must reach consensus on the answers or solutions. If students in a group do not reach consensus, they continue the dialogue until everyone on the team can agree. (15-20 minutes)

❖ **Sort the Items** is a strategy that promotes active investigation. The teacher asks students in teams to place ideas, concepts or statements on a topic in categories defined by the team. (5-10 minutes)

Cooperative Grouping for Student Engagement

❖ **Numbered Heads Together** involves students in cooperative discussion. The teacher assigns students to teams and then has students in each group number off. The teacher poses a question or a problem. Students work together on teams to answer the question or solve the problem. After about 8 minutes, the teacher calls out a number and then selects a team. The student with the number called, answers the question or solves the problem. (8-10 minutes)

Inside-Outside Circles is an engagement strategy that develops comprehension of content standards and expository text. The review of content vocabulary can also be done using this strategy. The procedures for implementation are as follows:

1. Every student is given a flashcard with a problem or vocabulary term on it.

2. Students line up. This can either be done randomly, according to height, length of name, etc. Then students count off in 2's.

3. The 1's will be on the *outside* of the circle and the 2's will be on the *inside* of the circle. The *outside* circle will face inward, while the *inside* circle will face outward. Each student numbered 1 should face a student numbered 2, as a partner.

4. Each pair will read the question on the other person's flash card and answer it. If the student misses the question, the person holding the card should explain the answer.

5. After giving an appropriate amount of time to answer the questions, the teacher tells students on the *outside circle* to move in a clockwise direction. The *inside circle* remains where they are.

6. The process of answering questions and switching is repeated until the *outside* circle has gone around once.

7. Students on the *outside* and *inside* circles can switch cards, move one position and repeat the process again (Kagan, 1994).

❖ **Mixed Up Summary** has students sequence what they have learned. The teacher writes key concepts or standards from the content lesson in random order on the whiteboard or overhead. Students unscramble the concepts and standards and reorder them in the right sequence. (5-8 minutes)

❖ **Graphic Summary** encourages students to make illustrations depicting the content information they have learned. Students work in pairs. They decide with a partner the key concepts they have learned and decide how to graphically represent them. (10 minutes)

❖ **Three Person Jigsaw** directs students to integrate pieces of information. Students in three person teams are each given a section of a text selection to read and summarize. Each student then teaches the main points of what they have learned to two other members of their study group and then quizzes them. (10 minutes)

❖ **KWL In Threes** can be used as and anticipatory set for content learning. Students in threes write what they *Know* about a topic to be studied. They then formulate questions about what they *Wonder* about the topic. After the *Teach* or direct instruction part of the lesson, the students circle the known information discussed, put stars next to the questions that were answered and add other information that they have *Learned*. (10 minutes)

Student Engagement Strategies That Allow Choice

❖ **Jet Traveling Pets** encourages students to consider alternatives and make choices. The teacher has students choose a travel destination for a pet to coincide with what they want the pet to do for entertainment. If they want their pet to play at the beach, they must choose a locale with a beach.

Students refer to travel itineraries to make the pet's flight arrangements. They explore travel brochures to arrange for the pet's entertainment. They peruse menus to decide on the pet's meals. They use geographical maps to decide on a locale. This strategy teaches students the expository reading standard of using charts and diagrams to find information. (15-20 minutes)

❖ **Frame the Questions** motivates students to create their own inference questions with a team. Students research the answers to the questions from the role the Team Leader assigns them. The roles include: internet researcher, text researcher, writer, illustrator and editor. (10-15 minutes)

❖ **Quilting Connections** has students graphically portray important concepts in a unit of study on a quilt. The quilt can be created with illustrations or graphics downloaded from the internet. Each graphic should represent an important concept that relates to the unit of study. (10-15 minutes)

Student Engagement Strategies that Nurture Higher Level Thinking

❖ **Inferential Questioning** nurtures higher level thinking and the learning of subject content. Higher level thinking questions require students to analyze, synthesize and evaluate information. The following are questions that can be used across subject areas to engage students in thinking about what they are learning.

Analysis Questions ask students to: disassemble information into discrete components, examine characteristics and define relationships.

> *What must you know for that to be true?*
> *What can you deduce from these facts?*
> *How can you categorize____?*
> *Which of these statements is not true?*
> *What do these things have in common?*

Synthesis Questions ask students to invent or create something new.

> *Can you describe this in a new way?*
> *What would you do if_____?*
> *Create a graphic representation for____.*
> *Make up a _____.*
> *Find a rule that describes this pattern_____.*
> *Combine these sentences to create_____.*
> *What would you predict from these facts?*
> *Integrate these facts to create_____;*

Evaluation Questions ask students to assess information in relation to a set of standards or criteria.

> *What is the common mistake in these_____?*
> *What types of characteristics do these have in common?*
> *What argument would you use to support the following claim?*

Student Engagement Strategies that Support Grade Level Content Standards Mastery

❖ **Turn to a Neighbor** is a strategy that can be used for quick feedback on students' comprehension of class or homework assignments. The teacher uses this strategy to check homework or content understanding.

As a homework check, the teacher writes a content statement on the board. The teacher then has students turn to a neighbor and tell the neighbor if he or she agrees with the statement on the board. If there is disagreement with the statement, the student must use the homework reading assignment to prove his or her point of view. (4-5 minutes)

❖ **3-2-1** is an effective strategy for finding out what students have learned from a content lesson. At the end of an explanation or demonstration, the teacher passes out index cards. The teacher has students write down *three* important terms or ideas to remember, *two* facts they would like to know more about, and *one* concept, standard or skill they have mastered. This task can be used as a transition from one subject area to the next. The strategy quickly gives the teacher feedback on what students have learned. (4-5 minutes)

❖ **Alphabet Connection** encourages students to develop the creative skill of idea generation. At the beginning or the end of a discussion the teacher gives each student a different letter of the alphabet. The teacher then asks students to think of one word or idea beginning with their letter that is connected with the topic that has just been concluded. (5-8 minutes)

❖ **A Note to a Friend** supports students synthesizing and organizing what they have learned. After explaining a content standard, after an expository reading or after a demonstration, the teacher asks each student to write a note to a friend. The note explains the standard, summarizes the expository reading or describes a process. (5-10 minutes)

❖ **Ticket to Leave** reinforces the important skill of reflection. This strategy can be used before recess or at the end of the day. The teacher passes out a printed ticket to students about the size of a half a sheet of paper. The teacher asks students to write the standards they learned and why learning the standards was important. Then the teacher asks students to write two additional questions about what they learned during the day or before recess. This strategy helps students understand that learning is never finished. (4-5 minutes)

❖ **Prediction Pairs** motivates students to formulate and validate predictions. The teacher asks students to take notes as they listen to a content presentation or a literature selection during direct instruction. The teacher asks students to share their notes with a partner to answer questions such as: *What will happen next in the story based on what you have heard so far? Do we need to divide or multiply to find the answer to this mathematics problem? What science principle do you think this experiment proves? What can you predict will happen in the future based on this historical event?* This strategy helps students use higher level critical thinking skills.

❖ **Double Check** engages students in peer editing. The teacher begins this strategy by putting students in pairs. The teacher designates one student in the pair to work on a standards-based assignment. The other student acts as a coach. The students exchange roles for the second assignment. At this point they ask another set of student pairs to *double check* their work. If the second pair agrees with their responses, the first pair continues to the next assignment. If the second team finds errors, the first team must correct their work before continuing to the next task. (15-20 minutes)

❖ **Review Partners** engages students in peer coaching. The teacher arranges students in partners. Partners review with each other the facts, standards or concepts they need to learn until they have mastered them. This strategy is effective for reviewing math facts, spelling words, grammar, geography terms and science principles.

❖ **Sum It Up** is a student engagement strategy that supports content standards mastery. The teacher uses this strategy by organizing students in teams of three after the *Teach* or direct instruction part of a lesson. The teams do one or more of the following: (5 minutes)

- Explain the main ideas of the topic.

- Web the important details that clarify the topic.

- Create responses to a hypothetical situation.

- List the attributes of a content standard.

- Predict what will happen if.

- List the consequences of the character's actions.

❖ **Benchmarking Work Teams** engages students in establishing their own goals for learning. The teacher gives students in selected teams the results of their benchmark tests. Teams list the standards that students on their team have not mastered. Then they design a plan to help their teammates master the standards. (15-20 minutes)

❖ **Standards Sum Up Journals** facilitates students mastering the content standards. The teacher gives pairs of students the daily standards. Students write the standards in their own words. They write what they know about the standards and what they need to learn. At the end of the day, students in pairs discuss the standards and what they learned. Then they sum up what they learned in a journal. (8-10 minutes)

❖ **Edit Response Groups** involves students in the important skill of peer editing. The teacher directs students to read and respond to each other's written work by: marking the passages they think are effective with a star; underlining what they don't understand or think is weak; circling errors in grammar, punctuation and capitalization. Students discuss their observations with the writer. Students can also use a standards-based writing checklist to edit each other's work. (15-20 minutes)

- ❖ **Ask Three Before Me** requires students to use the heuristic function of language. The teacher directs students to ask three other people in the class to explain something they don't understand before asking the teacher. This is important for the student asking and for the student explaining. The student who does the explaining actually learns the concept better. (10 minutes)

- ❖ **Trading Cards** engages students in reviewing the content standards. Students are grouped in teams of four after the direct instruction or *Teach* part of the lesson. Each team is given five index cards. Students on teams write one question on each card relating to the content the teacher covered. Teams exchange cards. Teams answer the questions and then return the cards to the team that wrote the questions. This strategy can also be used to review the ELA or math standards. Students can write a math problem on each card for the other team to solve. Students can write sentences that students must change to the past tense.

  Students can also write sentences using facts and opinions on the cards. The exchange team can decide whether the sentences are facts or opinions and give the reasons why. (15 minutes)

- ❖ **Dialogue Exchange** encourages students to master the skill of writing dialogue. Student pairs can write a dialogue between characters in a narrative. They can also create a conversation between a historical figure and a current day reporter. Students are encouraged to use quotations and correct capitalization and punctuation. (10 minutes)

- ❖ **Rally Table** focuses on shared problem solving. The structure of the activity can be set up in two ways. One way is to have members of pairs pass a piece of paper to and fro; taking turns to write ideas or answers to the open-ended problem the teacher poses. The other way is for each member of the pair to write his or her own answers or solutions. The partners then evaluate the solutions and together write up a new list of solutions. Pairs share their list with another pair of students. Together as a foursome, students integrate ideas and generate still another list. Finally, students work together to create a final solution or answer. (8-10 minutes)

Engagement Strategies that Monitor Accountability

❖ **Check and Connect Model** is a comprehensive student engagement model. The model has been developed for middle school students. The model has these components:

1. The model assigns a monitor to assist a disengaged student.

2. The monitor first establishes a relationship or *connects* with the disengaged student.

3. The monitor *checks* on the student's engagement by following up on school attendance and academic progress.

4. The monitor uses individualized intervention strategies to help the disengaged student develop habits of *Power Learning* (Christenson, 2004).

❖ **Student Contracts** monitor students' engagement in the learning process. A contract is made between the teacher and the student on an excel spread sheet. The student fills out the spreadsheet daily and confers with the teacher. As students improve the spreadsheet is filled out weekly. The purpose of Student Contracts is for students to perform a self-evaluation by keeping track of:

1. Number of assignments finished

2. Group participation

3. Homework assignments returned

4. Research projects completed

5. Time on task

6. School attendance

Interactive Electronic Media and Student Engagement

❖ **WebQuests** are powerful student engagement activities. They engage students in inquiry-oriented activities using information primarily from Internet resources. WebQuests extend learning through associated Internet links.

- WebQuests use Best Practice student engagement strategies of *scaffolding knowledge, using constructivist learning, using higher level thinking questions, using thematic activities and using authentic assessment.*

- WebQuests engage students in transforming knowledge into new understandings.

❖ **WebQuests** have the following components: *Introduction, Task, Process, Evaluation and Conclusion.*

Introduction: The introduction consists of a short paragraph that introduces the lesson or activity to students.

Task: The task describes learning activities. Sample tasks include: a problem to be solved, a position to be formulated and defended, a product to be designed, or a creative work. The task requires students to transform information.

Process: The Process includes the steps that students need to take. The process may include going to associated Internet links.

Evaluation: Assessment is usually done on a rubric. Students on teams assess themselves. The teacher also assesses teams.

Conclusion: The conclusion is the summary of the project (Dodge and Pickette, 2001).

The following are WebQuest sites:*

Best in WebQuests

http://bestwebquests.com

Web sites for Evaluation Rubrics

http://www.edb.utexas.edu/projects/allen/rubric.html

Web sites for content areas

http://www.zianet.com/cjcox/edutech4learning/cinco.html
(Cinco de Mayo, Cox, 2006)
http://www.kn.sbc.com/wired/China/ChinaQuest.html
(China)

Weather WebQuest and Weather Resources

http://www.weather.com
http://usatoday.com/weather/wfront.htm
http://www.earthwatch.com/index.html

*(valid at printing, 2010)

WebQuest Lesson Worksheet

Name: _____

Topic: _____

WebQuest Site: _____

I will complete a WebQuest named_____

and combine my problem solving skills with analysis of WebQuest

data to produce _____

Introduction:

Tasks:

Process:

Evaluation:

Conclusion:

Student Engagement and Project-based Learning

❖ Project-based learning engages students in *Power Learning*. Activities are interdisciplinary, constructivist-based and related to real world issues (Dodge, 2001). Project based learning:

  ❖ engages students in multidisciplinary research on the World Wide Web

  ❖ encourages students to create new paradigms of thinking

  ❖ motivates students to make real world connections

  ❖ involves students in meaningful dialogue

Steps for Project-based Learning

1. Decide on the project.

2. Decide on the amount of time for project completion.

3. Plan constructivist multidisciplinary activities with global connections or applications.

4. Create an Evaluation Rubric.

5. Introduce the project to students in small teams.

6. Have student teams complete the project within an agreed time frame.

7. Have student teams self evaluate on an Evaluation Rubric.

8. Reflect with students on what they have learned and how what they learned is connected to their global experiences.

Student Engagement and Lesson Planning

Lessons begin with a review and anticipatory set. Lessons have three parts:

TEACH   PRACTICE   APPLY

I. **Review** using the student engagement strategy *Turn to a Neighbor and* or *Pair Share*

    Anticipatory set focuses student attention on the content standards to be taught.

    Types of Anticipatory sets:

- Have students answer a question on a *quick write*.
- Use the *KWL* student engagement strategy
- Use the *Detective* student engagement strategy. Have students begin a lesson by finding information about the topic.

    Content Standard: Tell students the standard(s) they are going to learn. Tell students why it is important to learn the standard(s).

- Students need to restate the standard in their own words.
- Have students tell a partner why the standard is important.

    Examples:

> *Today we are going to learn about commas. This will help you punctuate your work correctly without constantly having to look in your grammar book.*
>
> *We're going to learn the classification system of plants, so you can correctly categorize them on the final exam.*

I. TEACH *Direct Instruction:*

- Information in the *TEACH* part of the lesson that is basic to students' understanding must be identified and scaffolded to enable students to see the relationship of each part to a whole (Hunter and Hunter, 2004).

- Model the information.

- Create meaning. Meaning is one of the most critical aspects of learning. Meaning does not exist in the material but in the relationship of that material to students past knowledge and experience (Hunter and Hunter, 2004).

- Use student engagement strategies throughout the *TEACH* part of the lesson.

1. Signaled answers

   - *Physical Responses* Thumbs up – down
   - *Response Cards*
   - *Turn to your Neighbor*
   - Make a plus with your fingers if you agree and a zero if you don't
   - Raise your hand each time you hear an example of _____

2. Choral response

   - *Students use choral reading.*
   - *Students repeat or chant a learning principle.*

3. *Think-Pair-Share.* The teacher poses a question to the whole class. Students discuss the answer in pairs. Then some individuals are called upon to share.

4. The teacher has students write a response on paper or on a *whiteboard.*

5. The teacher asks students to summarize what they have learned in a *Note to a Friend.*

II. PRACTICE

Students practice what they have learned after direct instruction. Practice is designed using five principles:

1. Engage students in practice by using student engagement strategies for content mastery including *Numbered Heads, Three Person Jigsaw, RoundAbout, 3-2-1, Mixed Up Summary, Inside-Outside Circles.*

2. Material should be practiced in *short meaningful chunks.* Practice sessions should be short to maintain focus and intensity. Teach one skill at a time (Hunter and Hunter, 2004).

   What implications does this have for teaching standards with more than one skill?

   ELA Standard: Identify and use regular and irregular verbs, adverbs, prepositions and coordinating conjunctions in writing and speaking.

   This standard has more than one skill. Therefore, the teacher should "chunk down" the standard and have students practice one skill at a time. Students can first practice regular and irregular verbs and then move on to adverbs, etc.

3. New learning needs *massed practice.* Old learning needs *distributed practice.*

   Practice periods that are close together are mass practice.

   Increasing time intervals between practice activities is distributed practice.

4. Practice with immediate feedback. Use *Whiteboards, Pair Share, Choral Response,* and *Cooperative Groups.*

5. Give specific knowledge of results. Set the criteria for acceptable performance.

III. APPLY

This is the creative construction part of the lesson. Students transform what they have learned.

1. Use *WebQuests* for research projects.

2. Use multidisciplinary *project-based learning*.

3. Use student engagement strategies including:
   Multiple Solutions, Send a Question, Team Research, Numbered Heads Together, and *Edit Response Groups.*

4. Use electronic media or group activities that extend higher level thinking including:
   Comprehension
   Application
   Analysis
   Synthesis
   Evaluation

Summary of the Elements of a Best Practice Lesson

1. Review previous learning.

2. Start with an anticipatory set.

3. State the standard and the reason for learning the standard.

4. **TEACH**
   • Present basic information in its clearest and simplest form.
   • Model through examples.
   • Use student engagement strategies throughout direct instruction.

5. **PRACTICE**
   • Used massed and distributed practice.
   • Use student engagement strategies.

6. **APPLY**

   Have students transform the information that they have learned.

Bibliography

Alvermann, P. (2002). Effective literacy instruction for adolescents. *Journal of Literacy Research*, Summer.

Anderman, L.H., and Midgley, C. (1998). *Motivation and middle school students*. (ERIC Document Reproduction Service No. 421281). Champaign: Illinois.

Anderson, A.R., Christenson, S.L., Sinclair, M.F. and Lehr, C.A. (2005). Check and connect: The importance of relationships for promoting engagement in school. *Journal of School Psychology*, 42, 2, 95-113.

Aronson, E. (2006). *Jigsaw classroom: Overview of techniques*. Web site: http://www.Jigsaw.org/overview.htm. (valid at printing, 2010)

Ames, C. (1992). Goals, structures and student motivation. *Journal of Educational Psychology*, 84.

Atkinson, J.and Kuhl, J. (2004). *Motivation thought and action*. New York: Praeger Publishers.

Bandura, A. (1997). *Social learning theory*. New York: Prentice Hall

Bellanca, J., and Fogarty, R. (1986). *Mental menus: 243 explicit thinking skills: A guidebook*. Thousand Oaks: Sage Publication.

Bellanca, J. (1982). *Student assessment, student behavior, motivation, teaching and learning*. Thousand Oaks: Corwin Press.

Bellanca, J and Fogarty, R.(1998). Learning: Mediating the challenge to change: In C. Brody and N. Danielson. *Professional development for cooperative learning: Issues and approaches*. Albany, New York: Suny Press.

Biehler, R., and Snowman, J. (1997). Teaching concepts: Cooperative learning. In *Psychology applied to teaching*. Boston: Houghton Mifflin.

Blank, W. (1997). Authentic instruction. In W.E. Blank and S. Harwell (Eds.) *Promising practices for connecting high school to the real world*. (ERIC Document Reproduction Service No. 407586). Tampa, Florida: University of South Florida.

Bligh, D.A. (2000). *What's the use of lectures?* San Francisco: Jossey Bass.

Bohm, U., Narciss, S. and Korndle, H. (2008). Developing mathematics and multimedia literacy through hybrid learning environments. *Distance Education, 4, 10.*

Bomia, L., Belluzo, et al. (1997). *The impact of teaching strategies on intrinsic motivation.* (ERIC Document Reproduction Service No. 418925). Champaign: Illinois.

Bonus, M., and Riordan, L. (1998). *Increasing students on task behavior through the use of specific seating assignments.* (ERIC Document Reproduction Service No. 422129). Chicago: Illinois.

Brandt, J. (2006). *Using Individual whiteboards for classroom instruction.* Perpich Center for Arts Education.

Bransford, J.D., Hammond,L. (2005). *Preparing teachers for a changing world: What should learn and be able to do.* New York: Wiley and Sons.

Bransford, J.D., McCarrell, N.S. (1999). *Rethinking transfer: A simple proposal with multiple implications.* Review of Research in Education, 24,1, 61-100.

Brewster, C., and Fager, J. (2000). *Increasing student engagement and motivation: From time on task to homework.* Portland, Oregon: Northwest Regional Lab.

Brittan, D. (2004). *Thinking lessons: New research investigates whether computer games can turn children into better learners.* Cambridge: Harvard School of Education.

Brooks, S.R., et al. (2001). *Improving elementary student engagement in the learning process through integrated thematic instruction.* (ERIC Document Reproduction Service No. ED 421274) Chicago: Illinois.

Carlson, R.M. (2003). *Experienced cognition.* New York: Erlbaum Associates.

Center for Talented Youth. (2002). *Listen-think-pair-share.* Baltimore, Maryland: John Hopkins University.

Cho, M. (2004). The strength of motivation and physical activity. *Youth and Society, 35,* 4.

Christenson, S. (2005). *Check and connect model: A model for promoting students engagement in school.* Minnesota: University of Minnesota.

Connell, J., and Klem, A. (2004). Relationships matter: Linking teacher support to student engagement and achievement. *Journal of School Health*, September.

Cornejo, Ricardo. (2006). *Eliciting spontaneous speech in bilingual students: Methods and techniques.* New Mexico: Center for Rural Education.

Cortese, E. (2004). The application of question-answer relationship strategies to pictures. *The Reading Teacher, 57,* 4.

Cox, C. (2008). *Cinco de Mayo WebQuest.* Web site: http://www.zianet. com/cjcox/edutech4learning/cinco.html. (valid at printing, 2010)

Croninger, R.G and Lee, V.E. (2004). National strategy for improving school connections. In *Wingspread Declaration.* Washington D.C.

Croninger, R.G. and Lee, V.E. (2001). Social capital and dropping out of school: Benefits to at-risk students of teachers' support and guidance. *Teachers College Record,* 103, 4.

Csikszentmihalyi, M. (2005). Emergent motivation and the evolution of the self. In D.A. Kleiber and Maehr (Eds.), *Advances in motivation and achievement.* Greenwich, Connecticut: JAI Press.

Cummins, J. (1980). The cross-lingual dimension of language proficiency. *TESOL Quarterly,* 14, 2.

Currigan, D. (2006). *Author's hotseat. WebQuest.* Web site: webinstituteforteachers.org/~btwilson/ gsotoquest_student_page.html. (valid at printing, 2010)

Dale, C., and Lane, A. (2005). *To interact or not to interact that is the question: An analysis of student engagement and online learning.* Web site: http://wlv.openrepository.com/wlv/ bitstream/2436/3109/1/Pages%2019-22%20To%20interact%20 or%20. (valid at printing, 2010)

Dodge, B. (2006). *WebQuests definition*. Web site: http://webquest.sdsu.edu/webquest.html. (valid at printing, 2009)

Dodge, B. and Pickette, N. (2001). *Rubrics for web lessons*. http://edweb.sdsu.edu/webquest/rubrics. (valid at printing, 2010)

Dodge, B. (1995). WebQuests: A technique for internet-based learning. *Distance Education,* 1, 2, 10-13.
Driscol, M.P. (1994). *Psychology of learning for instruction*. Masachusetts: Paramount Publishing.

Erickson, E. (1990). *Erickson's developmental states*. New York: Loose Leaf Library.

Erickson, E. (1968). *Identity, youth and crisis*. New York: W.W. Norton Company.

Felner, R.D., Jackson, A.W., Kasak, D., Mulhall, S., Brand, S., and Flowers, N. (1997). The impact of school reform for the middle years: Longitudinal study of network engaged in turning points for comprehensive school reform. *Phi Delta Kappan*, March.

Fillmore, L. and Snow, C. (2004). What teachers need to know about language. *ERIC Special Report*. Washington D.C.: Center for Applied Linguistics.

Finn, J.D., and Rock, D.A. (1997). Academic success among students at risk for school failure. *Journal of Applied Psychology*, 12, 97.

Frey, C., Meinholz, R., and Reed, M.A. (2006). *A quest for respect with the grouchy ladybug*. Web site: http://www.Yorkville.k12.il.us/webquests/webfrey/webfrey.html. (valid at printing, 2010)

Gawel, J.E. (2008). Intrinsic behavior. *Mil/firesbulletin*, 22. 25.

Gawel, J.E. (1997). Herzberg's theory of motivation and Maslow's hierarchy of needs. *ERIC Digest,* 18.
Glasser, W. (1986). *Educational psychology control theory in the classroom*. Massachusetts: Allyn Bacon.

Good, L. (2006). *Anthem: An utopian society*. WebQuest. Web site: www.washburn.k12.wi.us/high%20school/KirstenEnglish/Eng10/Anthem/anthemsustainableutopia/index.htm. (valid at printing, 2010)

Goodlad, J.I. (2004). *A place called school: Prospects for the Future*. New York: McGraw Hill.

Goslin, D. (2003). Engaging minds: Motivation and learning in America's Public schools. *Briefs on education research*. New York: Consultants Network.

Graham, S., and Weiner, B. (2006). Theories and principles of motivation. In D. Berliner and R.C. Calfee (Eds.) *Handbook on educational psychology*. New Jersey: Erlbaum.

Gunter, M.A., Estes, T.H., and Schwab, J.H. (1999). *Strategies for reading to learn think- pair-share instruction: A models approach*. Boston: Allyn Bacon.

Harmin, M., et al. (1998). Values and teaching: Working with values in the classroom. *The Humanist*, November.

Hattie, J. (2002). Student perception of preferred classroom learning environment. *Journal of Education Research*.

Henry, D., Henry, J., and Riddoch, S. (2006). *Whiteboarding your way to great student discussions*. Buffalo, New York: Buffalo State College Press.

Holzman, M. (1991). *Problems into problems: rhetoric on motivation*. New Hampshire: Boyton Cook Publishers.

Hunter, M., and Hunter, R. (2004). *Mastery learning*. Thousand Oaks: Corwin Press.

Instructional strategies online: What is think-pair-share? (2006). http://olc.spsd.sk.ca/DE/PD/instr/strats/think/index.html. (valid at printing, 2010)

Jablon, J., and Wilkinson, M. (2006). Using engagement strategies to facilitate children's learning and success. *Beyond the Journal Young Children on the Web*, March.

Johnson, R.W., and Johnson, R.T. (1999). *Learning together and alone, cooperative, competitive and individualist learning*. Boston, Massachusetts: Allyn Bacon.

Jung, C. (1974). *Dreams, reflections and memories*. New Jersey: Princeton University Press.

Kagan, S. (1990). The essential elements of cooperative learning in the classroom. *Education Leadership*, 47, January.

Keller, J.M. (1984). The use of ARCS model of motivation in teacher training. *Aspects of Educational Technology*, 84.

King, L. (1993). From sage on the stage to guide on the side. *College Teaching*, 43.

Klem, A., Connell, J.P. (2004). *Relationships matter: Linking teacher support to student engagement and achievement. Journal of School Health*, 74, 7.

Kohn, A. (1993). *Punished by rewards: The trouble with gold stars, incentive plans, A's, praise and other bribes.* Boston, Massachusetts: Allyn Bacon.

Kushman, J.W. (2000). *Increasing student engagement and motivation: From time on task to homework.* Northwest Regional Laboratory.

Lambert, W.E., and Peal, E. (1976). The relation of bilingualism to intelligence. *Psychological Monographs*, 5, 9.

Laosa, L.M. (2005). Bilingualism in three United States Hispanic groups. *Journal of Educational Psychology*, 94.

Lee, L., and Ursel, S. (2001). Engaging students in their own learning. *Canada Education*, Winter.

Long, T. W., and Gove, M. (2004). How engagement strategies and literature circles promote critical response in a fourth grade urban classroom. *The Reading Teacher*, 57, 4.

Lou, L. (2006). Conceptual and social cognitive support for collaborative learning. *Computers and Education*, 47, 3.

Lyman, F. (1987). Think-pair-share: An expanding teaching technique. *MAA-CIE Cooperative News*, 1.

Lyman, F. (2006). *Strategies for reading comprehension.* Web site: ReadingQuest.org. http://www.readingquest.org/strat/tps.html. (valid at printing, 2010)

Maclassic, D. (2006). *Whiteboarding in the classroom*. New York: Suny Buffalo State College Press.

Malone, M.R., and Lepper, M.R. (2003). Making learning fun. In R.E. Snow and J. Marshall (Eds.) *Aptitude learning and instruction: Cognitive and affective process analyses*. Hillsdale, New York: Lawrence Erlbaum Associates.

March, T. (2006*). What WebQuests are really?* Web site: http://bestwebquests.com/what_webquests_are.asp.

March, T. (2009). Will technology enable students to supercharge and personalize. *Bright Ideas for Education Newsletter*

Marks, H.M. (2001). Student engagement and instructional activity: Patterns in the elementary, middle school and high school years. *American Educational Research Journal*, 37.

Marzano, R. (2001). *Classroom instruction that works*. Virginia: ACSD.

Maslow, A. H. (1943). A theory of human motivation. *Psychology Review*, 50.

Maslow, H. (1987). *Personality and motivation*. England: Longman.

McBride, J., et al. (2003). Intrinsic motivation and achievement. *NEA teacher to teacher books*.

McCombs, B.L., and Whisler, J.S. (1997). *The learner centered classroom: Strategies for increasing student motivation and achievement*. San Francisco, California: Jossey Bass.

McDermott, P.A., Mordell, M., and Stolzfus, S. (2001). The organization of student performance in American schools: Discipline, motivation, verbal and non-verbal learning. *Journal of Educational Psychology*, 93.

Montesorri, M. (1967). *The Montesorri method*. Massachuestts:Robert Bently.

Motivating students to engage in class activities. (2006). Web site: http://www.nwrel.org/request/oct00/textonly. html#engage. (valid at printing, 2010)

Negeow, K., Kong,Y. (2001). Learning to learn: Preparing teachers and students for problem-based learning. *ERIC Digest*, ED 457-524.

O'Houle, C. (2005). *Learning theory and motivational styles.* Web site: http://www.learnativity.com/motivation.html. (valid at printing, 2010)

Patrick, H, Ryan, A and Kaplan, A. (2007). Early adolescents perceptions of the classroom social environment and motivation beliefs. *Journal of Educational Psychology,* 99,1, 83-96.

Perkins, T., Warzrak, M. (2006). *Authentic assessment: Mission possible or impossible.* Paper presented at the Conference Enhancing Teaching through Learning. Wisconsin: Wisconsin Education Council.

Piaget, J. (2001). *Psychology and intelligence.* New York: Routledge Classics.

Pintrich, P.R., and Schunk, D. H. (1996). *Motivation in education: Theory, research and applications.* Englewood Cliffs, New Jersey: Prentice Hall.

Pink, D. (2006). *A whole new mind.* New York: Riverhead Books.

Polyektov, Y. (2006). Bohm effect in superconsductors. *Low Temperature Physics,* 32,557.

Renchler, R. (1992). *School Leadership and student Motivation.* (ERIC Document Reproduction Service No. 346558).

Roderick, M., and Engle, M. (2001). The grasshopper and the ant: Motivational responses of low achieving students to high stakes testing. *Educational Evaluation Policy Analysis,* 23.

Roseman, S. (2006). *Poety Quest.* Web site: www.rccsd.org/rkeim/index.htm. (valid at printing, 2010)

Rubrics. (2003). Web sites: http://www.edb.utexas.edu/projects/allen/rubric.html. http://edweb.sdsu/triton/july/rubrics/RubricsforWebLessons.html. (valid at printing, 2010)

Rudell, R. (2003). Project-based learning. *Learning Technology Newsletter,* 3, 3, July.

Savery, J., and Duffy, T.M. (1995). *Motivation and perception in inquiry learning within a networked learning environment.* New York: Prentice Hall.

Savignon, S. (1972). *Testing communicative competence.* Montreal: Marcel Didier.

Schiefele, U. (1991). Interest, learning and motivation. *Educational Psychologist, 26.*

Schlechty, P. (2001). *Shaking up the school house: How to support and sustain education innovation.* San Francisco: Jossey Bass.

Seliger, H. W. (Ed.), (2004). *Classroom second language oriented research in second language teaching research methods.* Oxford: Oxford University Press.

Skinner, E., and Belmont. M. A. (1991). *A longitudinal study of motivation in school: Reciprocal effects of teacher behavior and student engagement.* Rochester, New York: University of Rochester.

Slavin, R. (2006). *Educational psychology theory and practice.* New Jersey: Pearson.

Stallings, J., and James, N. (2006). Learning to teach inner city diverse populations. Web site: http://wwwncrel.org/sdrs/areas/issues/educatrs/presrvce/pe3lk60.htm. (valid at printing, 2010)

Strahan, D. (2004). Promoting a professional collaborative professional culture in three elementary schools that have beaten the odds. *The Elementary School Journal, 104.*

Stuhlman, M., et al. (2002). Building supportive relations with adolescents. *Middle Matters,* Fall.

Terezini, P. and Pascarella, E. (2005). *How college affects students: Volume 2, a third decade of Research.* San Francisco: Jossey Bass.

Treadwell, M. (2003). E-knowledge. *Internet tools for Teachers, 7, 7.*

Tripp-Ervin, E. (1998). *Child discourse.* New York: Academic Press.

Vaca, A. (2002). *Learning and motivation.* New York: Academic Press.

Ventriglia, L. (2009). *Best practices in vocabulary development: The rule of three.* Sacramento: Younglighteducate.

Ventriglia, L. (1992). *Conversations of Miguel and Maria: How children learn a second language*. New York: Pearson.

Vygotsky, L.S. (1978). *Mind in society*. Cambridge, Massachusetts: Harvard University Press.

Wang, S., and Han, S. (2001). Six c's of motivation. In M. Orey (Ed.) *Emerging perspectives on learning and teaching technology*. Georgia: Idea Group Publishing University of Georgia.

WebQuests in action. (2007). Web site: http://www.spa3.k12. sc.us/WebQuests.html. (valid at printing, 2010)

What is brainstorming? Instructional strategies online. (2006). Web site: http://olc.spsd.sk.ca/DE/PD/instr/strats/ brainstorming/index.html. (valid at printing, 2010)

Wilburn, K.T., and Felps, B.C. (1983). *Intrinsic motivation and academic achievement instruction quality toolkit*. Massachusetts: Connect.

Willingham, W.W., Pollack, J.M., and Lewis, C. (2002). Grades and test scores: Accounting for observed differences. *Journal of Educational Measurement*, 39,1.

Yair, G. (2000). Reforming motivation: How the structure of instruction affects students' learning experiences. *British Educational Journal*, 26.

Zadina, H. (2007). *Brain research and language learning*. Presentation at English Language Learner Conference Washington D.C.: Department of Education.

About the Author

Linda D. Ventriglia is the Director of the Center for Teaching Excellence. Linda D. Ventriglia has a Ph.D. in Curriculum and Instruction and a Masters in Public Administration from Claremont University and Harvard University. She also completed three years postdoctoral research at Harvard in second language acquisition and literacy development. A former teacher and school psychologist, Dr. Ventriglia has served as an educational consultant across the United States and internationally. She has also served as Chief Consultant to the California State Legislature on the Education and Workforce subcommittee. Dr. Ventriglia is the author of *Conversations of Miguel and Maria: How Children Learn a Second Language (Pearson), Ready for English* (National Textbook), *Santillana Intensive English* (Santillana U.S.A.), *Teaching Strategies for the 21st Century*, and the *Best Practices in Education series*. Dr. Ventriglia has received a number of grants and has done national and international research on effective learning strategies. Dr. Ventriglia has also written a number of articles and has been featured in educational journals including the *California Educator*.